GRANDMA PREFERRED STEAK

And Other Tales

Gregory Clark

Infocor Limited, Montreal
Trade Distribution — General Publishing Limited

Foreword

The pieces in this collection are taken from a special body of Gregory Clark's work identified as The Packsack, a feature that appeared daily in many Canadian newspapers for fourteen years. The Packsack had a legion of devoted readers and was terminated only when a period of illness forced the author to give it up.

Greg described the Packsacks as *obiter dicta,* things noted in passing. But however transient an existence he may have assigned to the pieces when he wrote them, a large audience is now discovering them to be in all respects as fresh in the 1970s as they were when they rolled off the presses for their first million readers.

The first collection of Packsacks, "Outdoors with Gregory Clark," was published in 1971.

HUGH SHAW

Preface

This is the sort of book you dip into. My editors call it a bedside book. If you wake up grumpy, or go to bed grumpy, just dip in here, at random, and you may find a little relief, or possibly cheer.

Approach it the way you dip into a tray of canapés at a cocktail party; or if you are not the cocktail party type, the way you move from table to table at a Sunday School picnic, nipping up this and that.

I hope you find them tasty, or appetizing, to rouse your hunger for richer fare on any of the subjects here proffered.

Dip in.

GREGORY CLARK

Grandma Preferred Steak And Other Tales
by Gregory Clark
Edited and Compiled by Hugh Shaw

Copyright © 1974 by Gregory Clark
Gregory Clark is an associate editor of Weekend Magazine

Published by
Infocor Limited
Information Services Division
Michael S. Baxendale, Director
245 St. James Street West
Montreal, Quebec

Trade Distribution in Canada
General Publishing Limited
30 Lesmill Road
Don Mills, Ontario

ISBN 0-88890-024-4

Cover and illustrations by Jack Tremblay
Design — Max Newton

Printed and bound in Canada

Contents

Grandma Preferred Steak

On the bus, a man asked me if I had seen any hawks this year on their big September migration. I said no, but I had seen a flight of a hundred and fifty black bellied plover going south in August, a magical sight as they lifted and hissed through the air low over my head.

"My grandmother," I said, "who was born in 1840, lived in Toronto and she told me of the stupendous flights of wild passenger pigeons going over the little city sometimes all day long, millions of them in a silent flow like smoke from horizon to horizon."

There were marshes on both sides of the town and wild duck, geese, shore birds like plover and snipe, streamed across the Toronto sky. And in spring and fall every provision shop, butcher, grocer, had festoons of wild game hanging by his door, and in fall, deer hung by the windows.

10

In Grandma's day the supply of game seemed inexhaustible. Indeed, I remembered, in my youth and until very recently almost everyone ate game in season. Twenty years ago, when a man came home with a dozen or so ducks or partridge, he used to distribute them among his friends. When a deer hunter arrived home, he had his buck cut up by the family butcher and immediately made the rounds of his friends, giving away roasts, steaks and chops. Those days are going, if not gone, forever. The game now goes into the deep freezer. And the sportsman has his game over the entire winter. For example, I can't imagine anything more beautiful than a New Year's Day buffet, with a cold roast turkey on it, a haunch of cold venison, three or four roast partridge and a couple of brace of cold roast wild ducks. That and some red currant jelly, and maybe some wild grape jelly, and a platter of thin bread and butter, and you've got a New Year's layout ready for a royal visit.

"Yes," my fellow passenger was saying, "We've been beef eaters for comparatively a short time. Beef was too hard to transport. Not enough land was cleared for extensive pastures. Until our fathers' time, we Canadians were pork eaters. A cow has one calf. A sow presents us with ten pigs. Pork and game were our grandparents' proteins."

And I remembered how little my Grandma cared for a treat of venison or game. She liked sirloin steak.

Shortcomings and Goings

For Christmas, my wife gave me the first beautiful blue flannel blazer I have ever owned. Very handsome garment, with the badge of my old first-war regiment, long disbanded, worked in flamboyant gold thread on the left breast. A moose head, with radiant horns.

It must be forty years since I owned a navy blue or other dark suit. Early in life, I took to Harris tweed for a jacket with lots of pockets, and gray flannel pants. The blazer was as novel and exciting to me as a plug hat to a Zulu.

But shortly I found my wife and friends starting to brush my shoulders off, every time they looked at me. Indeed, strangers at gatherings of any kind that I graced in my new blazer, would take automatic little whiffs of their hands at my shoulders. And on looking into the matter, I discovered with some humiliation, that my shoulders were usually sprinkled with what could be nothing else than dandruff.

I went straight to my barber. He was outraged at the suggestion that I had dandruff. His examination of my thatch bore him out.

"Now," he said, "I will tell you what you've got. You've got tall friends."

I admit I am only five foot two and sixteen-seventeenths inches.

"Your tall friends," he said, "flick their cigarette ashes on you. They've been doing it for years, and you never noticed, in tweeds."

From now on, I am standing slightly apart from my tall friends. It is humiliating to think of one's self as an ashtray, blazer or no blazer.

Cricket

A good deal of a person's character and temperament may be based on experiences of early childhood that lie beyond the rim of memory and recollection. It is good, therefore, to have an elderly auntie who can remember what a brat you were and can supply you with data of immense importance with regard to defects of character that secretly baffle you. For example, nothing bores me more than hockey games, football, baseball, horse races. Wherever great throngs of excited and happy people are assembled to watch a handful of athletes perform, I find myself filled with a queer, unreasonable sense of irritation and distress. Until an old auntie pulled the veil away for me, thirty years of my life had been spent with the secret impression that I had a nasty anti-social streak in me.

"I can see you," my auntie taunted, "being dragged off to the cricket matches. . . ."

"Cricket!" I protested. "In Canada?"

"Oh, yes, your daddy," said auntie, "was the demon bowler of the old Parkdale Cricket Club and they played every Saturday afternoon somewhere or other. So your mamma dressed you all up in your little sailor suit and dragged you down to the cricket matches, where you had to sit on her lap, hour after hour, the long, dopey, cricket afternoon through."

I could feel weights falling off me as she spoke.

"I'd forgotten my father played cricket," I muttered. "I knew he golfed, bowled. . . ."

"It would be before you could remember," auntie said, "But how you hated it!"

Cancelled

"Letters I Never Posted" is the name of a book I may write some day.

When I was a young man, I took tremendous affront at something that was done to me. I have happily forgotten what it was. But I sat down and wrote a letter that would have fairly frizzled the offender.

I read it to my father. He was enthusiastic. He made some useful suggestions for small changes, and offered me a few powerful phrases for incorporation. I re-wrote the letter. It was a masterpiece. But when I read it, in its improved draft, my father had still better suggestions, and still more damning and lucid phrases. I wrote it out again.

"That's perfect!" my father cried, when I read it over to him. "Perfect! Now chuck it in the basket."

"Chuck it . . .?" I gasped.

"Certainly. It's served its purpose," said my father. "You have got it off your chest. You feel a great deal better now. Chuck it in the basket."

Which I did, and learned at an early age one of the great secrets of a happy and healthy life. A hundred, maybe three hundred times in my life, though I am a writing man who can get a great deal off his chest in the ordinary course, I have written a Letter Never to be Posted. It is a lot of fun. It is gratifying to the very soul. I have told off my friends, my enemies, public men of the highest rank, foreign rulers, also small store keepers and my neighbors across the street. I have even written small quick letters to my wife and my mother-in-law, and these I usually tore up and flushed the little pieces down the toilet.

But among the Letters Never Posted were some good ones, too: one to Mr. Churchill at the end of the war; some love letters; some letters to friends, the kind of letters you should write on New Year's Eve. And never, never post.

Economy

A new oil lamp wick is from five to six inches long. In due time—and a good long time it is—the wick burns away and becomes so short that it will not reach down into the oil in the lamp unless the bowl is full. I have seen my grandmother sew the new length of lamp wick onto the old.

Thus you save from three to four inches of perfectly good lamp wick. When you come to the joint between the new and the old wick, and it will not turn through the slot, you are forced to throw away the remnant of the old wick, maybe an inch.

Lamp wick costs a few cents a yard. In my grandmother's day, it cost a tenth of its present price. At the time my grandmother was effecting this economy and many others, we were not poor. We had chenille curtains between the dining room and the hall. We had at least two barrels of Northern Spies in the cellar. I had as many as four shirts, which is two a week, washday being Monday. I had a Red River coat. My grandmother knitted me mitts to match; scarlet. My father was a well-to-do man. He was an editor. He earned $27 a week. Mr. Norris, the druggist at the corner, did not call him Joe, in the familiar manner he employed with other customers. He addressed him as Mr. Clark. Mr. Norris knew his society.

But my grandmother sewed the old lamp wick to the new. And she could cut a man's coat down to fit a boy so that even the boy could see no evidence of the deception. Never a bone went out of the house that had not been boiled white. If salt were spilled, for what is the fat side of the palm but to wipe the salt back into the salt cellar? If milk turns sour, what is better than tea biscuits? My grandmother was a soft-spoken, valiant woman. She never wasted a penny and died penniless.

Mother Tongue

A woman who came to this country as a child of twelve from one of the Hebrides could speak nothing but Gaelic when she arrived years ago.

She never forgot her Gaelic as the years passed, and she would amuse her children singing songs in the old quaint tongue, and her sons and daughters grew up with snatches of Gaelic phrases to toss about on St. Andrew's Day. All her life, the mother spoke English with the faint accent of the isles still on her tongue. But she raised her family to be Canadian to the bone.

In her early seventies, the mother took a stroke and went to hospital. When she was well enough to speak, she could not speak or understand a word of English, but only the Gaelic. By some strange trick of the mind, affected by the stroke, she was thrown back across the years to her childhood mentality.

And her sons and daughters, when they came to see her, had to bring an interpreter with them who could speak the

17

Gaelic. They were fortunate in finding a nurse from the isles.

It is not the first time in medical records that a stroke has deprived people of memory. But this case had elements of sheer romance about it. The middle-aged sons and daughters gathered about the sick bed, with the nurse functioning as an interpreter for the astonished old lady on the bed.

They told her of her life in Canada, the nurse converting their story into the mysterious and ancient tongue unknown to them. The old mother asked unintelligible questions, and the nurse translated them to the children. Finally, the old lady smiled shyly at them all around.

"She says," translated the nurse, "she does not believe a word of it, but that you do indeed look like her kin."

Good Men Who Fly

The bush pilot has won a deserved reputation in the rapid opening of Canada's formerly inaccessible resources of the north. His courage and ingenuity, and above all his remarkable capacity for daring improvisation, are legendary in the northland.

But all that differentiates him from the rest of the

frontiersmen, when you come to think of it, is his vehicle, the airplane. Our bush pilots are merely the latest edition of the explorers, prospectors and adventurers who have enriched our country from the time it was first discovered. They went by canoe, pointer, dog-team. And their feats were no less romantic than those of the bush pilots. It simply stands to reason that when the airplane was invented, there were already the adventurous men who would take it into that wild and challenging country where they had been performing miracles with far humbler vehicles; the sled, the canoe and the scow.

When we speak of bush pilots, we might also mention the bush doctors, the bush parsons who, for a century and more have been quietly carrying on their work on the frontiers. We have put the emphasis on the word pilot. It should have been on the bush. For if there had never been aircraft, it would be a safe guess that about ninety-five out of a hundred of the men who became bush pilots would have been up somewhere in the bush anyway.

In a conversation with Archdeacon Clarke of James and Hudson Bay, I remarked that it took a good man to go into the north country.

The archdeacon who drives dog teams, who can mend broken bones as well as souls, who will saw or haul or shovel or carry packing cases for you without the loss of any of his venerable dignity (he is only a boy in his forties) looked thoughtful.

"Put it this way," he amended. "It takes a good man to stay in the north."

Bush pilots are just good men who can fly.

Good Men with Horses

The small-town doctor of my boyhood, around 1900 to 1910, usually kept a pair of horses and sometimes four. A pair of good drivers, a good buggy horse and possibly a saddle horse.

The doctor lived in one of the mansions of the town or village. At the back was this good stable equal to calls as much as twenty, thirty miles away.

The care of his transportation was of course too much for the doctor, so he employed one of those Englishmen who were in such liberal supply back in the nineteen hundreds. During the summer, the doctor's son was stable boy. That was his vacation job. But when September came, the doctor would look out for a likely Englishman, fresh arrived from overseas, and hire him for the winter. Nearly all Englishmen either knew about horses or pretended they did. It worked out about the same.

They stayed until June. And then, with their winter's savings, they would head West. And the doctor's son, home from school or college, would take over the stables again for the summer. Thousands of doctors' sons all over the country will remember this. Thousands of Englishmen, long,

long since Canadians, will remember their first jobs in the new country as stablemen to Canadian country doctors. It was an institution, part of the building of Canada.

Those Englishmen in such liberal supply in the early nineteen hundreds had no advance booking of housing or employment. All they had, when they arrived here, was a queer old suitcase of green or brown Willesden canvas, a peak cap, a tight fitting tweed suit and a pipe in their teeth.

The doctors' sons of those days who shared the responsibility for the horses with them, recollect those Englishmen with considerable respect. They were steady, responsible characters, a little shy and a little astonished. When June came, they tucked their wages tightly in small wallets and picked up their queer old suitcases and headed West. Canada was building in the early nineteen hundreds.

The Truth About Paul Bunyan

Once more on a coast to coast television broadcast of a Rose Bowl football game Minnesota has made another barefaced attempt to claim Paul Bunyan as an American citizen and a denizen of the State of Minnesota.

Everybody of any consequence in the world knows that

Paul Bunyan was born on the shores of the Bay of Fundy and is a Canadian through and through. It was in New Brunswick, years and years before he got as far as Minnesota, indeed it was in the year of the Blue Snow, that Paul found the Baby Blue Ox in a cave. As far as Minnesota is concerned, Paul had to log off all of New Brunswick, Quebec, Ontario and Michigan before he arrived, in the full glory of his career, with Babe the Blue Ox by that time forty-two axe handles and a plug of chewing tobacco between the horns, to swipe the timber off Minnesota the way a haymaker cradled the crops off the cleared fields in Paul's wake. He logged off Minnesota in one measly winter.

About the only claim Minnesota has on Paul is the fact that it was in that state that the idea occurred to him to develop a new technique in lumbering, whereby he removed the pine, stumps and all. Thus he was able to proceed the following winter onto the Canadian prairies and the Dakotas, employing this new technique, with the result that you can hunt the prairies from end to end without finding a single stump.

Minnesota had better get its facts straight.

Big Devil

We do not realize the authority the surveying profession has enjoyed, during the exploration of our great country in the matter of giving names to townships, lakes, rivers and even mountains. I can picture the average surveyor in earlier days, carrying a pencilled list of names in his pocket, including those of his wife, children, relatives and friends, all of whom would rejoice to have their names inscribed on the map of Canada.

Flying over the north country in a bush plane, I recognized a body of water I had known many years ago, which enjoyed the noble name of Big Devil Lake. This name came from an Indian whose home and trapping headquarters it had been before the white engineers came through. The Indian's name was Chief Big Devil.

A few years ago, when a job of resurveying was done, the name of the lake was calmly changed to Annie Lake.

Annie is an awful name for a lake of such rugged beauty and ancient charm as Big Devil. I do not know who Annie was; doubtless a lady of charm. But probably she was the wife of the boss surveyor who also had the job of naming or renaming many of the townships around Big Devil. I imagine he was a punctilious and even a courtly type. For he named townships Roosevelt, Truman, Dieppe, Caen. This gives a clue as to the time of the renaming.

For right smack in the middle of all these namely townships, and not very far from Annie that used to be Big Devil, is the township of Stalin.

As the plane soared past, I thought I detected the ghost of a smile on the face of Big Devil Lake.

Monster

A cabin maid in a Great Lakes steamer saw a monster that made the front pages all across Canada. It was at least forty, maybe a hundred feet long. Its head stood up from the water and had long horns or ears that flapped horribly.

It was a dirty brownish color, suitable to something dug up from the nether depths. It writhed and twisted across the surface, kicking up a spray as it travelled. A ghastly new sea serpent.

I have seen several of these monsters. They are flocks of young mergansers or fish ducks. A family of mergansers will number twelve or fifteen. As soon as the nestlings can travel, the mother duck leads them to join up with neighboring families. It is not at all uncommon to see fifty to seventy-five mergansers in one flock, with half a dozen adult females among them and the rest "flappers," which is the correct name for young ducks not yet able to fly.

When they are still too young to have been taught to dive after fish, the young mergansers form a procession, a long line of forty or more of them. I have seen a hundred and twenty in one flock. At the head of the snake of birds, head to tail, rides a female who regularly rises on her end and flaps her wings vigorously. At intervals in the single-file procession other adult females are stationed, and occasionally they too rise and give their wings a few beats. On an oily evening sea of the Great Lakes, it required little imagination to convert this procession of fish ducks into a sea monster with horns at its heads, ears flapping, and waving its fins now and then down its long and grisly length.

The most petrifying sea serpent I ever saw, apart from a German submarine, was a driftwood pine tree. Its bark was worn away, until it appeared slimy and greasy as it wallowed in the slow waves. Its roots stuck up, gray and horrible, like horns. I fired five shots into it, from a high velocity rifle!

Red Cedar

How superstitions start was explained to me by an Ojibway and his explanation seems to be suitable to all races and climes. No Ojibway will burn red cedar in his fire. To do so brings certain disaster.

"Do you believe this?" I asked the Ojibway.

"Well, I don't believe it, but I don't burn it," he explained. "In all our Ojibway country, the red cedar is generally a strange looking tree. It will grow on strange places, like barren rock islands and points where even a pine won't stand. It has a different look. And anything that looks different is important to Indians.

"Its wood has perfume. Back in olden days, therefore, red cedar became important in our eyes. So perhaps some chief or wise man announced that red cedar must not be burned. To do so would bring bad luck. It is interesting, it is nice, to have beliefs of this kind. It makes life more interesting. It gives subject for talk among people without many subjects for conversation.

"But look: it needed proof. It was all very well to have a rule. But it must be proved. So sooner or later, along would come some reckless man. He would be reckless and careless in all things, in his canoe, his hunting, his quarrelling. Many times he should have had bad luck before he burned red cedar. Other reckless men before him had died of bad luck before they burned red cedar. But that was because they were reckless in their canoe, their hunting, their quarrelling. This man I speak of who is reckless in all things and is going to die of it anyway hears that it is unlucky to burn red cedar. And he burns it. Then the bad luck that was coming to him anyway, because of his general recklessness, comes. This is the thing we have been waiting for maybe for generations. But the rule is proved now. We can name the man, and remember the man. It was because of his recklessness he burned the red cedar. But it was his other recklessness that brought him disaster. Nobody remembers that. Everybody remembers that he burned red cedar.

"I do not believe in superstitions. But I don't burn red cedar. It reminds me never to be reckless."

Companions of a Special Order

A good many of those tens of thousands of Canadians who are summer travellers to Britain and Europe will be visiting the military cemeteries to pay commemorative respect to sons, brothers, friends.

The cemeteries are beautifully kept. Many of them are on hills or slopes, and so devised that you do not come on them suddenly. You have to pass through a quiet gate, with a little toll house beside it, where you must pay the toll of searching through a little book, an index, which will show you precisely where, up yonder, past the glossy hedges, beyond the perennial borders that already have an ancient and tended look, you will find whom you seek.

No matter how loved and unforgotten he may be, you will not find him as easily as you think. For you have not taken many paces past the flowers and suffered the first shock of perceiving in what great company he lies, maybe three hundred, maybe a thousand, before you are suddenly gripped with a most curious consciousness of intrusion. There is something monastic about a military cemetery.

It is not the silence, not the flowers, so various and unpatterned, not the smallness of the identical stones. But long before you find the section and the row and the numbered plot, the realization keeps swelling in your mind that he is not alone and has never been alone. Captains and corporals, colonels and privates, they do not lie, they stand, and have stood for year upon year. Not strangers, as we will be when we take our place beside utter strangers, but companions of a special order of men. And when you find your

28

man, and fall on your knees in sudden unintended tears, it is you who are alone, and he that is in a great and watching company.

You say your prayers, you struggle in an agony of memory, and you leave. But you leave with the strangest feeling of having intruded.

The Years of Night

In the first great war, we faced east, the Germans faced west. Every day we faced the sunrise. Every day they faced the sunset.

It has always seemed to me that this had a profound effect on the morale of the two mortal enemies. Unlike the last war which the tanks and aircraft brought out into the daylight, the first great war was largely a night war. The infrequent battles began at dawn, subsided to a sort of stupor during the day and came to a blaze again as dusk fell. But between the battles, the long years of trench warfare were years of night and terror.

As the night paled and comforting day drew near, we lined our trenches and greeted the sunrise. When the comforting day waned and the perilous night drew on, we lined our trenches again and the Germans faced the sunset and saw the night fall as we did not. There is something foreboding in every sunset.

Realistic people will scoff at the notion that so trivial a thing as sunrise or sunset might have an effect on the fate of nations at war. But of the million men on each side facing, on the one hand, sunrise, and on the other, sunset, an extremely small proportion were realistic. Most were the sons of Adam. They were the heirs of countless generations of superstition and a lingering folklore.

It stands to reason that realists should be industrial and political leaders, our educators and our men in control generally. So it may be that they are incapable of comprehending the mystery, half way between the light and the darkness, in which the mass of mankind lives. Around my neck on a string, for forty-eight years, I have worn a small stone with a hole in it. My grandmother told me, when I was a child, that such a lucky token would keep me from being killed by the arrow that flieth by day or by the pestilence that walketh in darkness. So far, she has been right.

30

Motives

A very moving documentary motion picture is the film story of the division made up of captured Russians in the last war. They were employed by the Germans against their own country and the sad end of the story, after the German defeat, is the packing up of the division in a sealed train which carried the troops back to Russia and Comrade Stalin.

Makers of documentary films find it hard to let the picture speak for itself. They like to lard the film with interviews with notables whose comment is supposed to enrich the picture. In the case of this Russian tragedy, the authorities who were presented discussed most learnedly just what motives led the captured soldiers to enlist with the Germans. Some were for anti-communism. Some for anti-Stalinism. It was astonishing to hear these scholars and politicians trying to define the political motives of soldiers.

You have to be a soldier yourself to know that the prime motive of soldiers is to be with their buddies. Not all their comrades-in-arms. Just a little clique of buddies that every man belongs to in his section or platoon, or at most his company. An army may have high and resounding motives. A division may be addressed by its commander in most eloquent terms. But it is not a division or a battalion that goes into battle. It is an agglomeration of little cliques and squads and groups of half a dozen men who just like to be with their boon companions in a predicament the making of which none of them had a hand in, and the large significance of which escaped them at the moment.

The Gamblers

Mr. Ralph Allen, editor (in the 1950s) of Maclean's Magazine, invented a new gambling game in Italy, called Snore Roulette.

I was the roulette. Due to my age and infirmity, I have gone to bed early for the past sixty years. And in some of the billets we occupied as war correspondents it was necessary for as many as ten or fifteen of us to sleep on the floor of one single room.

Being gifted as a sleeper, I can sleep on a floor, or sitting up, or even standing. And deep in my sleeping bag, in my cosy corner of the billet, I would be hard at it by eight o'clock or not later than nine. By hard at it, I refer to the snore.

On my mother's side, I inherit a highly individualistic

snore. There are those who snore steadily, stroke on stroke, like a mill wheel, all night. There are those who snore to a pattern like the trombone score in a symphony, loud passages here, soft passages there, with long intervals of just sitting with your trombone on your knee. But my snore is pure erratic. It starts immediately after sleep comes, which is usually two minutes. And it keeps up until shortly after I am waked. It starts high, or it starts low. It goes maybe three snores and then a sudden snort, or it may go fifteen snores and then a strangle. But upon the snort or the strangle, there is a brief pause for station identification, and I start on the next series. There is no telling how many snores I will go. That is the essence of gambling.

And it was Mr. Allen who perceived its possibilities. Since nobody else wanted to go to bed at 8 p.m., and since bridge, cribbage or even chess was out of the question under the circumstances, Mr. Allen conceived the idea of betting on how many snores I would go on each cadenza. You placed your money on the table, taking a number from three to fifteen, as a rule. When the bets were up, they called the start at my next snort or strangle. And the number of snores I went won the pot. I am informed Mr. Allen once won two thousand seven hundred lire on me. That was twenty-seven bucks.

Flashes

There is an old belief that when a man is drowning, his whole life flashes before his eyes. I was talking to one of the ship's officers of an ocean freighter that had come up the St. Lawrence seaway during which venture he had fallen overboard at one of the locks and very nearly drowned. I asked him what his thoughts were as he felt himself going.

"The only thought I had," he said, "was about my false teeth. If they fell out, how awful I would look when they found me."

This recalls my own experience some years ago when I was upset while trout fishing very early in the season, less than a week after the ice had left the lake. Between nearly drowning and nearly freezing to death, I had a narrow escape. All I can remember thinking about, as I felt unconsciousness enfolding me, was that my wife had put two pairs of fur-lined snow boots on the attic stairs for me to take up and put in the cotton mothproof bags for the summer, and I had neglected to do so. What worried me was that my wife would find those boots still on the attic stairs.

I have talked to several dozen soldiers who got half way through the pearly gates when desperately wounded, and the things that passed through their minds during the half-dark of final realization were almost invariably preposterous. The pick of them all was that of the sergeant whose last conscious effort was quickly adding up the money owed him by four or five of the boys in his platoon, drawing a line and sighing: "A hundred and ten francs!"

34

September Incense

I would like to tell you about my grandmother, Louisa Greig and her three friends, Auntie Turnbull, Mrs. Armour and Mrs. Malloch. My memory places them as very old and venerable ladies in black satin, sateen and lustre, with bonnets encasing their tidy old heads, they all being widows.

I suppose they were in their sixties. It was their custom, all through the year, to meet every Wednesday at somebody's house: the home of a niece, nephew, son, daughter, and when they ran out of these, they elected the home of some close friend of any of their families.

They arrived carrying their aprons and pet cooking utensils, such as a favorite paring knife or a measuring spoon, in their black satin shopping bags.

After greetings, they proceeded at once to the kitchen and took over. They took over for the whole day, for the doggonedest jamboree of cooking you ever imagined. It was their hobby, their recreation and their joy. These four old ladies, in an unobtrusive way, were endeavouring to keep alive the ancient Canadian culture they had inherited from the pioneer ancestors. Cookery, fifty years ago, was one of the larger aspects of our culture. A cultured home in Canada was one in which you got a great big square meal.

Of course, at pickling time, when redolent September dawned, there was quite a lot of feuding in our various families. The Wednesdays had to be given up by the merry quartette, because Grandma Greig was seized upon by one or other of her immediate daughters or daughters-in-law for the whole pickling fortnight. And the other three ladies suffered a like imprisonment by their kin.

It is happy and it is sad to recollect them now. When you

35

walked along the September streets of our cities, towns and villages, the very air was heavy with the incense of pickling. I used to think of it as the autumnal incense our homes sent up in thanksgiving to God for the harvest. You can walk the streets now in September and never get a whiff of vinegar or spice, never a faint savor of chili sauce or mustard pickles, no hint of gherkins in brine, no brain-tickling token of tumeric or enamelled red peppers.

And doubtless the factories which have taken over the production of all this autumnal incense worked out some efficient system by which they extract all the by-products of their fumes.

No incense rises.

Aunt Lib

Aunt Lib is the last of her numerous generation and the repository of a thousand famous recipes. Grandma Greig's oatmeal cookies, rhubarb marmalade, devil's food cake which was so wonderful its ingredients could never be written down, mustard pickles of such incredible subtlety that you could not tell if they were vinegary or elusively sweet, and which made all meat, whether ham, beef, lamb or sausages taste exactly 100 per cent better, net.

Aunt Lib has all these and countless others in her keeping. She got them from her mother, and my mother, and all her other sisters, cousins, and aunts, not to mention friends and relations from Halifax to Victoria.

But, alas, the recipes are not recorded. For Aunt Lib belongs to the generation that not only did not need to have recipes written down, but if they were written, they were never followed. What was great or noble in a recipe eluded the written word. It was mystic. It was a gift.

Now, when Aunt Lib is growing a little old, it is amusing to listen to her grandchildren and great-grandchildren trying to rescue for posterity some of the secrets of the golden age of cookery.

"Well, let's see," says Aunt Lib. "You take flour . . ."

"How much?" checks the modern.

"Whatever is needed," explains Aunt Lib, patiently. "And butter . . ."

"How much butter? A tablespoon, two tablespoons?"

"Well, of course, that depends on the amount of flour you're using, doesn't it?" laughs Aunt Lib, kindly. "And a little baking powder . . ."

"But look!" wail the moderns. "You have to tell us the amounts."

"How can I tell the amounts?" says Aunt Lib, still patient, "Unless I am doing it."

So she does it. And the moderns gang around ready to document it. But so swift are her hands, so deft a pinch of this, a dab of that, a little wisp of the other, that the moderns surrender, as they surrender when they see Margot Fonteyn dancing, and realize that some things are beyond the reach of science, record, documentation.

To Light the Hearth

Fall is the time of the year for open fires. Maybe in February they are more dramatic to come in to, from a harsh grey day. But October fires on the hearth are more sentimental. They are the first needed fires of the coming winter. In front of an October grate, you can renew the ancient marital vows between man and fire.

There is considerable argument in literature as well as among our contemporaries as to which kind of wood is the best for a fireplace. The early Canadian writers praise birch, because, while it is a hard wood, and burns long and hot, it is also a quick wood that kindles fast and makes a roaring fire in a few minutes. Birch was also praised by the pioneer writers because it burned down to a glorious cherry red ember. And in the days not a hundred years gone when most of our cooking was done right on the hearth, the bed of ruby and enduring embers was rightly praised.

But now that open fires are almost one hundred per cent ornamental and sentimental, there is one wood praised by the old timers that moves into first position: and that is, pine roots.

When you get a pine root or chunk of stump going on the hearth, there is no rush or hurry about its fire. The flames are individual, quiet if not actually lazy. They are deep orange in color, and lick delicately at the stump as if reluctant to let go. No blaze seems to want to stay in the fireplace like a pine root fire. Next to embers, a pine root fire is the most perfect contemplative fire of all. Paul Bunyan knew this. That is why, when he logged off the prairies, he pulled the pines up, roots and all.

Soupe aux Pois Forestière

Nolin Trudeau, who is well and warmly known to news-papermen and advertising men all across Canada, is an authority on what lumberjacks ate in the good old days.

"All a lumberjack was provided," says Nolin, "was beans, flour, molasses and tea. Anything else he wanted, he had to bring into the lumber camp with him or get it out of the bush around. Real shanty beans, in the old lumbering days, consisted solely of two parts beans and one part pork. No molasses, or onions. Just solid beans and pork in that classic proportion. And when the beans were done, a bowl of brown sugar would be tossed on top, and then served. The lumber-jacks brought in with them, in their packsacks, any deli-cacies such as the brown sugar, the pork, or any other fix-ings, which were jealously shared.

"When Christmas came, the lumberjacks were let go home for the holiday. They took their empty packsacks with them. They would snowshoe fifty, a hundred miles. Their wives, mothers or sweethearts would have ready for them, to take back in, a firkin or tub of frozen pea soup. For prior to Christmas, they would have been making boilings of pea soup, the real stuff, the kind you eat with a fork, not a spoon. And each batch would be added to the tub hung outside to freeze. This tub or firkin was the shape and size of a packsack. After the Christmas celebrations, the lumberjacks would head back for camp. And every man carried that lump of frozen pea soup in his pack, it having been broken out of the tub.

"Back at camp, they would go out and break or chop off a hunk of frozen soup from where it was hung on the outside of the shanty and melt it. This was a great relief from the pre-Christmas routine of beans. It had sentimental value, too, for these lonely men. They vied with one another in praise of their personal pea soup."

"How do you know all these wonderful things, Nolin?" I enquired.

"Did I ever tell you," replied Nolin, "the recipe for braised porcupine à la térébenthine?"

"Térébenthine?" I checked.

"Turpentine," translated Nolin.

Mallards

Somebody presented a niece of mine with a brace of beautiful wild ducks, mallards.

"What on earth," she phoned me, "do I do with them? They're raw!"

"Raw?" I said.

"They've got all their feathers on, and their insides in," she squealed.

"Well you pluck them, and then you draw them," I outlined.

I then learned that she had never drawn or defeathered a fowl in her life. She is a grown woman with several children. And on a little further enquiry the astonishing fact emerged that hardly any young woman in city or town in the present generation connects a hen scratching frowsily around the barnyard with the beautiful pallid, smooth, nude bird she buys, all done up tidy in cellophane, at the supermarket. She knows some weird and wonderful transition must occur, like that of the crawly caterpillar transfigured into the lovely butterfly. But who does it, how it is done, she doesn't know and has no wish to know. It is all part of the mystery and magic of the modern way of life. She is shielded from the unpleasant particulars. To her, a hen in a barnyard is one thing. The chicken in cellophane is another. The connection between them is so remote as to be negligible.

"Well," I said, "there are firms that specialize in dressing fowl. You can take your ducks down to the market and have them plucked and drawn for about a buck."

"Uncle Greg," she pleaded, "you like wild duck, don't you?"

"Indeed I do."

"Then, if I bring them over . . ." she suggested.

Thus I came by a brace of mallards, and I took them down to the market and had them plucked and drawn for about a buck.

41

Decline of the Goose

My father, who had a very poor head for lullabies, used to sing me to sleep as an infant with a strange collection of songs, one of which went:

> It is my opinion
> That stuffed with sage and inion,
> No bird that flies
> Is half so nize
> As a goose with sage and inion.

As I was singing my grandchild to sleep, this one emerged out of the long past, and it called to mind the fact that the goose has declined almost to the vanishing point, as the bird of celebration in Canada. In former times, it was the goose that was the centre of the feast at Christmas, New Year's and even Thanksgiving. Not the turkey, the chicken, the duck or the glazed ham, but the big, wide, fat, brown glistening goose. Though we may have got the idea of Thanksgiving Day from the Americans and taken with it their Pilgrim Fathers' turkey, it was some generations before the turkey took over this country from the traditional goose.

One reason for the popularity of the goose was that it could be raised around the barnyard and it behaved comfortably, feeding itself off the pasture, whereas turkeys had to be penned or else ran themselves skinny after grasshoppers. A reason for the decline of goose was that it was pretty rich fare for increasingly sedentary generations.

Now that even the farmers are mechanized, appetites are less Eskimonian, and go more for pallid victuals than fat ganders.

Oysters

Looking down at her plate in the smart restaurant to which we had taken her, Auntie Beth, of our family, who comes from Texas, said in all humility:

"I can't thank the Lord for oysters!"

So she skipped saying grace, and said it double the next morning for breakfast.

But she ate the oysters, with an expression of distaste that even large gobs of condiments, tabasco, horse radish, spicy tomato chili sauce and lemon, in quantity increasing with each oyster, could not help her to dispel. My feeling is that there are not enough oysters in the world to justify us in urging people to eat them. If they don't like the look of them, okay. Agree. Admit they are ghastly. If they don't like the slipperiness of them, fine. Pretend to have a little trouble yourself in picking your oyster up with a fork. If they gag when they get the oyster in their mouths, lean over and suggest that maybe they are allergic to oysters. Then reach across and take the plate from them.

When Franklin Delano Roosevelt died, there was still an R in the month (as if that mattered), and I had to work on the story of his funeral all over such epicurean regions as Washington, New York and other cities of the Atlantic seaboard. The press photographer with me had never really encountered oysters in their native habitat, and when I took him from fish house to fish house of great name all up and down the coast still faithfully reporting the story of the great man's demise, I found I had released an oyster glutton upon the world. At the rate at which this photographer consumed oysters, there would be none left for mankind at large. So I took him into Joe the Oysterman's place in New York and ordered Mattatucks for him. This, I figured, would cure him of his unholy passion. Mattatucks are oysters about the size of a felt insole for a size nine workboot.

He ate a dozen and a half, and when he called for more, I sent for the head waiter and had my friend thrown out of the joint for disorderly conduct.

Oysters call for a nice middle approach, in which you should never encourage and occasionally discourage, for the common weal.

Canaypes

One of my country friends who quite accidently made himself a millionaire by lending a friend a few hundred dollars to file some mining claims, quit school, as a boy, before he tried his high school entrance. Some people with a million dollars would be a little embarrassed by their educational or cultural shortcomings. But not my country friend.

He threw a small party for some of his bosom companions lately, and when the floor waiter arrived at the hotel room, very reverent, with the menu, my old rowdy-dow country friend said:

"We'll start off with some canaypes."

The waiter, who I think was Czech or possibly Ukrainian, never turned a hair.

"Canaypes, sir!" said he, correctly, making a notation on his pad.

Not canapays. The world is full of people with not fifty dollars to their name who take great solace of the fact that they can pronounce canapé with the true, the Gallic accent. Each to his solace.

"Why," enquired my friend, "do they call them little doodads canaypes? One-bite sandwiches! Biscuits with cayviar on them!"

I didn't know, so we sent for the dictionary, down in the hotel library. It said: "Canapé: a thin piece of bread, toast, etc., spread or topped with cheese, caviar, anchovies or other appetizing foods. See Canopy."

So we looked up Canopy, and it said: "A covering suspended or supported over a throne, bed, etc., or held over a person, sacred object, etc. An overhanging projection or

shelter. Archit., an ornamental rooflike projection or covering. The sky."

My seventh grade millionaire friend said: "What the Sam
Hill!"

The more you investigate some things, the dimmer they
get. So I sent for the French dictionary. And all it said was:

"Canapé—sofa."

"Aha, that's it," my friend cried, illumed. "Things you
eat sitting on a sofa."

And that's the way we et 'em.

Terrific

In the new office building, the walls and partitions were of
aluminum. Aluminum and glass. The effect was strangely
breathtaking. To offset or puncture or splinter the strange
chill of aluminum, the designers of the building had spotted
the modernistic chairs with bright colored cushions; the
stagily spaced settees and benches were upholstered in
orange, light green, rust red, gas blue. The strangely spec-
tral tone of the tall aluminum walls was broken, at random,
by slender drapes of soft beige and cocoa and ground white
pepper.

"Aha!" was all I said.

"Tremendous, isn't it?" said the architect.

"It must be hard to work here, in these offices," I ventured, "at first."

"Do you know," countered the architect, "that the working efficiency of the junior staff of this office has been stepped up as high as thirty per cent, as the unquestionable result of these surroundings?"

"How," I asked, "about the old boys? What has been the effect on them . . .?"

We went into the manager's office. It was terrific too. His windows gave him a panorama of half the great city. His walls were nearly all window. The rest was aluminum, draped with long shrouds of liver-blue, spleen-green, brain-grey.

"It's marvellous," said the manager. "I can't keep my mind on my job. I keep looking out the windows all day. If I don't I get the jimmies."

"There, now," soothed the architect, pressing the manager back into his lovely soft-functional fungus-colored chair.

"It's terrific," sobbed the manager.

To be modern you've got to be young.

Classified

For at least fifteen years, a man whom I first knew as a youth but who is now clothed with the dignity of a rather precocious middle age has been waiting on me in my favorite hardware and ships' chandler shop. Over the years, he has assisted me in groping through dark bins in the remoter fastnesses of the warehouse for merchandise of rare description and unusual size: grommets which I required to repair an Austrian rucksack, copper three-inch nails when they were right off the market, galvanized hooks and eyes for tent flaps, a tracking eye for a canoe, copper tips for cracked paddles, a sea anchor, which is a sort of cone-shaped bucket for towing astern or amidships to keep the craft drifting slowly the way you want it—these are only a few of the things my old acquaintance has helped me to find in a chandler's shop, which is naturally the most jumbled emporium on earth.

He is a slow-going man, but reliable.

The other day, after we had successfully run to earth a double Spanish burton, I decided to find out his name.

"Look, old boy," I said, "we've known each other a long time now. You call me Greg. What'll I call you?"

"Mr. Henderson," said he.

War of the Razors

The war between the various safety razor manufacturers has been going on so long that it deserves to rank with the Thirty Years War or the Wars of the Roses. It has been one of the greatest perennial battles in the advertising world for almost as long as most of us who shave can recollect. Millions of dollars have been spent in the effort of these companies to cut each other's throats with a safety razor. Obviously they haven't succeeded because they are all at it as strong as ever, with no signs of any blood having been lost. And they have provided us who, of course, pay for the advertising in the end, not only with good shaving equipment, ever improving, but also with zestful advertisements which encourage us to shave and enjoy shaving. It's inspirational.

But the latest campaign in the long razor war is based on speed. Speed in changing blades. One company came out with a sensational campaign featuring zip, swish, click, snap, bingo! It's in! It's out!

This speed had all the other razors gasping on the ropes

for a few months. But now you will see that all the other warrior razors have come up with speed. It's out! It's in! Flash, zip, whip, snap, snip!

You would think from this that we shavers are all in a terrific hurry. The picture this razor campaign conjures up is of the manhood of the nation racing madly into the bathroom, snatching the razor off the cabinet shelf and, after slapping some sort of rapid, brushless cream on their faces, proceeding in a blur of motion, to swipe the whiskers off their chins.

The truth of the matter is, about eighty per cent of men love shaving. They like to fiddle and diddle around with hot water, soap, lather and a razor, the more amusing the mechanism the better. A shave is like a daily resurrection of Lazarus. A bristly, stubbly, clammy man goes into the bathroom. A shining knight comes out. The only kind of people who shave the way the razor advertisements imagine people do are the kind of people who write safety razor advertisements.

Heretic

In a cigar store, I was astonished to overhear the following conversation. The customer said:

"A packet of cigarettes, please."

"What kind?" enquired the girl behind the counter.

"Oh, it doesn't matter. Any kind," said the customer.

The young lady, born and raised in the age of submission to brand-name advertising, was completely at sea for a minute. She turned and faced the racks of cigarettes and fumbled helplessly while she made up her mind. Finally she selected a widely advertised brand and handed them to the amused customer.

"They're all the same to you, are they?" I asked the customer.

"Aren't they to you?" he retorted. "I can't tell one from the other. I notice that when anybody offers anybody else a cigarette, they always accept it, and seem to enjoy it. I've long ago ceased being choosey in this life. One good motor car is as good as another, one good hat, one good kind of soap—they're all good."

Both the young girl behind the counter and I were deeply

shocked by the heresy being uttered by this cheery stranger. He was striking at the very roots of advertising, of business, of our basic way of life, vocal, vociferous, clamorous, suppliant.

"Then you don't believe in advertising?" I suggested.

"I sure do. I am in the advertising business," said this dangerous man. "All advertising does is prove that one thing is as good as another. If it were not so, there would be no need for advertising. Everybody would know that one thing was better than others. I suppose advertising does serve a useful purpose in forcing the makers of things to make them good, but the other function of advertising is to attempt to sell one good thing in competition with another good thing."

He was just tearing the cellophane off his newly bought packet. I offered him one of mine from my case. He smiling accepted. I held my lighter for him. He took a pull and nearly choked his head off.

"Hand rolled," I explained, "from some tobacco my uncle grows at the back end of his vegetable garden."

The Chuckinout Method

When you think of all the vast quantity of goods being bought every day in all the big department stores, in all the medium sized stores in downtowns in hundreds of cities and towns all over creation, and all the thousands of small stores in the uptown streets and the crosstown streets and the suburbs and their shopping plazas and supermarkets, the question is: where in heaven's name is all the stuff accommodated? Are there enough new housing enterprises going up in all directions to take in all this vast amount of merchandise?

The food, of course, is consumed, the clothing in time wears out. But think of the furniture, the furnishings, the appliances, the hardware, the tons and tons of almost imperishable goods that are being whisked into and out of all those legions of shops and stores wherever you look. Where does it go? Why are not all the houses we see bursting? Where do the books go, the tons of books that are bought daily?

When, in a word, will everything be full up, no more room, and nothing more sold?

A merchant of my acquaintance who delivers several tons of assorted merchandise from his store every day says:

"Well, in our house, we have what we call a Chuckinout Day every three or four months. We chuck out a lot of stuff to make room for more."

Without periodic Chuckinout Days, I suppose our entire economy would collapse.

Paper Plates

At our summer cottage, we use paper plates. Only when we have nobby guests, which is rarely, do we use the china. And after each meal we sit back and say:

"Whose turn is it to burn the dishes?"

It is not economical, as far as money is concerned. It costs around $10 or $15 for the summer supply. But it is highly economical of holiday time, since dish washing is confined to a few pots and pans.

A couple of summers ago, we ran short of paper plates and I wrote to the department store in the city with which we do most of our shopping and ordered three hundred plates. A week went by. Then ten whole days. The summer was fast passing. And there had been a lot of tiresome dishes to wash. So I wrote to the merchandise manager of the big store, whom I know, demanding to know what had happened to my order. He was away on holidays so I didn't hear from him for another two weeks.

However, in the same mail I sent another order couched in these terms:

"To whomever opens this letter:

"Under no circumstances permit this order to get into Normal Channels. Take it immediately to the saleslady in the paper plate department on the main floor who, being about forty years of age, wears usually a dark flowered print dress. Ask her to pack up three hundred paper plates, address them to me in her own hand, take them up to the Post Office in your store, which, for your information, is on the third floor, northwest corner. Ask her to charge the necessary stamps to my account. If you fiddle with this order as you have done with a previous order sent ten days ago, you will lose my account for keeps. Just do what I demand in this letter, and no more fooling."

We got the paper plates two days later.

We got the first order five days later.

They had been in what are called Normal Channels, which is a sort of canals-of-Venice system which large businesses construct for their own convenience.

Any business that consults its own convenience ahead of that of its customers is not in business at all as far as I am concerned.

The merchandise manager, catching the whim of the thing, sent me at the conclusion of his holidays an enormous "pack" of internal correspondence showing how a whole bevy of dreamy clerks had channeled my order through shopping service over to mail order, back to shopping service, with several twenty-four hour delays in this department and that.

And by golly, all this time we were washing dishes.

Business as Usual

In the army before a battle we used to speculate furtively and privately on the possibilities of the morrow: who would survive, and who would take over? Colonels and seconds in command did not often go west, so there was little likelihood of large, dramatic consequences. It was the company commanders and lieutenants among the officers, and the sergeants and corporals in the ranks who were the subject of speculation. There was no use speculating if you counted yourself among the casualties, for in that case it wouldn't matter. But as a rule, battles came and went, and there wasn't much change in the situation. Whoever was left did fine.

In a thriving business with which I am acquainted, three deaths among the top executives occurred in the past year. In business as in the army, there is always the private and furtive element of speculation as to the shape of things to come. The three deaths were thought to make a dramatic shake-up in the organization. But as far as I can see, everything is going on as usual in the business.

With what humility do the dead withdraw. Like figures in an antique drama, they fold their hands and bow backwards out of our memories, their faces hidden more with every backward pace until, in shadow, they are forgotten except by an effort of the mind. In business as in the army, the reinforcements are right at hand.

Breakfast Ham

In the hotel dining room I was having breakfast with a local surgeon who had already performed an operation and was taking a break. Surgeons seem to prefer to operate as soon as they wake up, fresh.

Into the dining room came two very important looking gentlemen. They were dressed in what you might call super-executive type suits. They were groomed like princes. Cold-eyed and glancing neither right nor left at any of the other breakfasters, indeed, as though nobody in the room were worthy of a glance, they signalled to the head waiter where they wished to sit, and proceeded to a table. Standing, they had a brief colloquy with the head waiter who signalled a bus boy. The bus boy obediently vanished out the door. The gentlemen sat down. The bus boy returned with some telegram forms and stationery for which he had obviously been sent.

When waitresses approached, they, without raising their heads, waved them away. They wrote telegrams, both of them. After a few minutes, the larger and more elegant of the two raised a finger and summoned the head waiter. The head waiter, bowing, summoned a waitress. Breakfast was ordered without reference to the menu which the waitress proffered.

"There's a couple of visiting moguls," I mentioned to the surgeon.

"No," he said, glancing at them. "They're a couple of local real estate men."

"They're putting on quite an act to impress the audience," I submitted.

"No, to impress themselves."

"Each other?" I asked.

"No, each one is trying to impress himself," said the surgeon.

Deference

While sitting in the office of one of my cronies who is an advertising agency executive of high rank, I witnessed an interesting procedure.

His secretary came in the room, shutting the door behind her.

"It's Mr. Whiffle," she said.

"Ah!" exclaimed my friend. "Switch 'em, quick!"

The secretary hurried over to the wall and removed a framed photograph. She carried it over to an ornamental bookcase, the bottom drawer of which appeared to be stacked with framed pictures. Hastily sorting through them, they fished one out and replaced in the drawer the one she had taken down. Then she hung the new picture on the wall.

"Show him in," directed my friend.

Mr. J. T. Whiffle, of the Whiffle Pickle Corporation, one of my friend's large accounts, what they call in the advertising business a six figger account, came in, a presidential personality. I was introduced and took my departure, but before going I took note that the picture newly hung was one of Mr. Whiffle, taking his place on the wall with the Queen, Mr. Diefenbaker and Sir Winston Churchill.

The Lesser Tycoon

Getting tough, several of our Canadian cities have recently decided to double the fine for parking in prohibited and restricted sections of downtown streets. Doubling fines, however, won't really solve the problem, for there are people to whom fines mean nothing. And prominent among them are the big-shot businessmen who simply put their fines on their expense accounts. They never feel it personally. I was driven to a meeting by one of these lesser tycoons. He is a man for whom I have the highest respect as a fly fisherman and a business bulldozer. But his social attitude leaves much to be desired. He drove to the door of the building we were about to visit. It was after 4 p.m., and the signs on the lamp posts clearly indicated that there was no parking allowed after 4:30 p.m. I called his attention to the fact.

"Don't give it a thought," he assured me, as we left the car.

Our meeting lasted until well after five o'clock, and several times I reminded my friend of his car parked outside in a prohibited area.

All he did was make soothing gestures.

"Look:" he said, as we put on our coats to depart. "We go out. There's a ticket on the windshield. Five bucks. Suppose they have doubled the fine. Ten bucks. I give the ticket to my secretary. She sends a cheque in. And charges it to my expense account. It's charged to car operation."

"But that," I protested hotly, "is defeating the whole purpose of traffic management. And besides, you are charging your fines back on the public. That's who pays your expense account, in the goods they buy . . ."

"Son," said my friend, "when you've been in business as long as I have . . ."

We went outside. My friend's car was gone.

He stood up to the traffic constable at the corner and reported it.

"That?" said the constable, waving his arms to the traffic. "The police tow truck took it away about 4:45. You'll have to go to the police garage, at the west end of the city . . ."

My irate friend telephoned aldermen, local members of parliament, several ward heelers.

They just laughed at him. It's the only way to handle lesser tycoons.

The Hang-Up

When I answered the telephone ringing, a crisp female voice demanded:

"Mr. Clark?"

"Yes!"

"Hold the line a moment."

I held the line a moment. I held it two, three, ten moments. The two guests in my room sat silent, our conversation suspended.

Not a sound on the phone.

One of my guests raised his eyebrows at me.

"She told me," I advised him, "to hold the line a moment."

Time passed.

I could feel my gorge rising. I could feel the flush coming up out my collar. I was just on the point of banging down the receiver when there was a little click.

"Sorry," said the crisp female voice, "but Mr. Zushpak has just stepped out of his office."

"Mr. Who?" I yelled.

But she had hung up.

Now, I realize that Mr. Zushpak belongs to a very large constituency of gentlemen of affairs who have this habit of telling their secretary to get them Mr. So-and-So on the line. I suppose it is a generally accepted practice amongst all who rate a secretary. And I have no doubt that amongst themselves they are prepared to sit and wait whenever a brother gentlemen of affairs puts them to this indignity. It would be interesting to try to survey just how many hours of the big business day are wasted by gentlemen of affairs waiting upon the convenience of fellow gentlemen of affairs.

But I think the only decent thing a gentleman of affairs can do when he wants to telephone somebody who is not a gentleman of affairs, is pick up the phone and do the job on a man-to-man basis. And what's more, from now on, when anybody tells me to hold the line, I am going to hang right up.

Slippery

One of my acquaintances who is general manager of a fairly hustling organization recently faced one of those crises which recur in most businesses when everybody suddenly gets stupid, slovenly, dopey. What brought the crisis to a head was the disappearance of a valuable technical book, one of those loose-leaf volumes with a slippery plastic cover.

The general manager, who had borrowed it from a competitor, forwarded it by office boy to one of the other offices in the company. It never arrived although it was a matter of about fifty feet in distance.

Nobody had seen it. The office boy vowed he had delivered it. The secretaries of the subordinate denied they had seen it. A search, not unlike a spring cleaning of the entire premises failed to discover it. Finally, there it was, sitting on top of the office mail box.

Ah! Then the girl who was commissioned to deliver it to its proper destination, let it slide, in its slippery cover, undetected, from the bundle of files she was carrying. It got kicked under a desk. It was lost again. When it was recovered, the boss called a full meeting of all the staff, from second-in-command down to office boy.

"Who," he roared, "do you think you are working for? Yourselves? I'm the general manager. And even I am not working for myself! Now, snap out of it."

When he got the book back, he took it home for safe keeping until he could return it personally to his competitor.

His wife threw it out with the garbage along with a lot of other junk she found scattered around the living room.

The Gripe

The man who comes and fixes our TV set every time it gets out of kilter was in a state of high indignation when he called. He had just come from a house occupied by a family of new arrivals from Europe, and they had roused his ire.

"The woman scolded me," he said, "for the poor workmanship of our Canadian appliances. She assured me such clumsy workmanship and such second-rate materials would never be tolerated where she came from. After she pointed out all the weaknesses of the TV set, she took me into the kitchen and showed me her refrigerator with its defective door latch, then she raised and lowered windows to demonstrate how badly they were fitted. Canada, she says, knows nothing of workmanship. Such things as these would never be tolerated in Europe."

"So I suppose you called her down?" I suggested.

"I had to hold myself," the repair man admitted. "I don't want to be fired for being saucy to customers. But I did agree with her, as politely as I knew how, that she had made a great mistake in coming to Canada instead of staying in Europe. I admitted that Canada was a very flimsy sort of country, and I supposed, after another few months of it, she would be going back to a country where workmanship was workmanship."

"What did she do?"

"She gave me a dirty look and showed me the door," said the repair man. "What gripes me now is all the things I could have said to her and didn't."

"Such as?"

"Aw, the heck with it," said the repair man. "Let's have a look at this TV set of yours. How many times is it I've been here?"

"Six," I said.

The Locksmith

The locksmith who came to mend some locks at my house arrived with nothing more than a screwdriver and a small round box for squirting powdered graphite into the locks.

He said that ninety per cent of all lock trouble could be fixed with these two tools. And he was sick and tired of lugging a big tool box around with him.

"Locks," he asserted, "are probably the best built bits of mechanism in modern use. They're simple and solid. The reason they go wrong is generally due to screws being allowed to get loose. If a man took a screwdriver once a year and went around tightening the screws that hold the locks in place, he would never have lock trouble.

"The second cause of trouble," remarked the locksmith, "is oil. If a lock gets sticky, the women get the little oil can and dose enough oil into the mechanism to keep a bicycle going six months. That oil gums with dust. Then you've got a sticky lock for sure. These little packets of powdered graphite cost only a few cents. You squirt the powder into the lock, and she's as slick as silk. . . ."

The locksmith took his screwdriver and removed the whole business from my door. He examined it critically, twisting and turning the parts.

"H'mmm," he murmured. "Just as I feared. A broken tumbler. It rarely happens. . . ."

So he had to get in his car and go back to his shop for the tool box. When he returned, he took the lock all apart and poked and scrabbled through the tool box to see if he could find a part to replace the broken tumbler.

"As I feared," he said. "This is an old-fashioned type . . . I'm afraid you'll need a new lock on there. . . ."

Which I did. And after he had screwed the new lock into place firmly with his screwdriver, he took the graphite squirter and gave it a good dose.

The Greeters

A chartered accountant who, in his long life, has had occasion to be on intimate terms with a great many businesses of almost every description, from large industries employing hundreds, down to small legal or insurance firms employing a dozen people, tells me that employers and executives who are strictest with their humbler employees are those most recently risen from the humbler ranks of business and are most conscious of the fact.

"As a rule," he says, "I can tell by the way an executive speaks to his minor employees whether he has been up in the brass section ten years or twenty. The real crisp ones are the five-year tycoons. Elevator men, junior clerks, filing clerks get short shrift. Your five-year tycoon hardly sees them. He is pretending they are not there. Ten-year tycoons are short and snooty with everybody below the rank of head bookkeeper and stenographers of less than ten years' service with the organization. But around fifteen years of executive rank, he begins to feel socially secure. By that time he is usually a vice-president and a director, and he finds it a little difficult to distinguish between the elevator man and his fellow directors. He greets them all with equal warmth. Which is zero."

"You seem prejudiced against executives," I suggested.

"Aw, the poor devils," said the old auditor.

Hustle

A university professor who was recently persuaded to serve on the committee of a well-known social service organization had his first experience of meeting some of our city's leading businessmen on their home ground. The committee met, as a rule, in the offices of one or other of the big executives who were fellow members with the professor on the governing body of the society.

"I can't help but notice," the professor told me, uneasily, "the air of forced enthusiasm that prevails in these big businesses. When I come to a meeting, I have to be introduced to the colleagues and the bright young men of the business in which my committee colleague is usually president, or vice-president. And invariably there is that quality of forced enthusiasm, a sort of radiation of energy that expresses itself in the way they all speak, or seize your hand, or stare at you with extraordinary intentness. There is something hectic about it . . ."

I had to put my professor friend straight.

"That is not forced enthusiasm," I assured him. "That is the normal air of big business. It is real enthusiasm. It is energy. It is pep, vigor, drive. If you don't encounter that queer impression of forced enthusiasm, you are in a business that is not quite on top of the heap. Modern big business attracts to its upper levels only the most energetic, slightly frenetic types."

The professor stared into space a moment.

"Is that where they go?" he remarked softly.

"Who?"

"All those hustlers we get at the universities," the professor explained, "who haven't got time to listen."

Up A Back Stair

A considerable number of our big stores and large businesses can't be bothered.

They can't be bothered doing anything more than exchanging what they've got for your money. Here's the goods. Take it or leave it.

Some young friends of mine banded together to buy a tiara of brilliants for one of their number who was going to her first big social event in her first really smashing party gown. The ornament for her hair cost $30. They found it in one of the most fashionable shops. It was exactly what they wanted. It was beautiful. It was imported from England.

But it didn't quite fit. So they went back to the shop, the day before the party, and asked what could be done to make it fit. Could it be bent a little? Could, perhaps, a couple of tiny extensions of some sort of flat steel be soldered on the tips, to make it cling to the beautiful head of the girl to whom they were presenting it?

Of course not. The sales girls, salés ladies, if you please, were mildly amused at the idea. You may have your money back, of course, they said loftily. The manager was consulted. He regarded the enquiry as ridiculous. We have the goods. You have the money? If it doesn't suit, here's your money back. The idea that they should take any further interest in the transaction was too preposterous for consideration. My young friends were abashed.

But they hung on to the tiara and went to a small jewelry shop on a side street. There an old gentleman with his spectacles on the top of his forehead gave them the address of a handyman he knew who could fix anything in the way of watches, clocks, musical boxes, rings, brooches, chains.

Up a steep stairs to a dark cluttered room they climbed, where an amiable old man, for one dollar, soldered on two short bits of spring steel and made the tiara fit like a halo.

There is always somebody prepared to be bothered, which is a good thing to remember when you almost find what you want in one of the unbotherable establishments.

Just look around the corner, or up a steep stairway some place.

Keeping the Faith

Now and again divine justice exerts itself in a fashion that is worthy of special note.

A Canadian man of affairs who died three or four years

ago had become very wealthy by dedicating himself to the pursuit of money in a way that estranged not only nearly all his fellow citizens but also his own family.

There was nothing wrong about his methods of acquiring money. It was his terrible passion for it that made him rather gruesome to the beholder, even though most of us will stand on our heads for a worthwhile profit.

He divided his wealth among his children, and among the provisos of his will was the command that he be cremated. When the ceremonies were over, the crematorium officials enquired as to the disposition of the ashes. Since the law firm in charge of the estate had attended to the execution of the will insofar as the cremation was concerned, the enquiry was directed to them. The lawyers consulted the will and found no directions as to the disposition of the ashes, so they telephoned the children to enquire which of them would like to take the old gentleman's dust.

Nobody was interested. Not one of them. They told the lawyers to do what they liked with the ashes.

Now, lawyers are a cagey lot. You can't just chuck the ashes of a wealthy old man into the waste basket. After several attempts to induce some member of the family to undertake at least a little responsibility in the matter, the lawyers solved it in a characteristic fashion.

They went to the old gentleman's bank, rented a safety deposit box, put the ashes in it. And there he rests, where he longed to be.

BEEZAWEEZAWEEZA

"As absurd stories can be told of me," wrote the famous essayist Michel de Montaigne in the sixteenth century, "as of any man living." And Montaigne had no motor car to involve him.

The silliest situation in which we can find ourselves is when we get into one of those instantaneous rages that come to us while motoring, when another car offends us, and we glare angrily into the face of some old friend.

"You infernal fathead!" I exploded, when a car came swooping out of a stop street and had to swerve violently to avoid a collision with me. Our two cars screeched to a stop with fenders touching. In a towering fury, I opened the barrage while my eyes were still fixed on the fenders. "Can't you read? Don't you know what a stop sign means . . .?"

And then I looked into the flushed face of one of my oldest friends and lifelong fishing companions.

"Well," I said, limply, "you're a fathead, anyway!"

My old friend never opened his mouth. But there was a glint of indignation in his eyes.

My engine had stalled in the confusion, and I was busy with the starter.

"You've got to watch out for those signs," I pursued, just for something to say. "If I hadn't been awfully nimble, we'd have had a bad . . ."

Beezaweezaweeza went my starter.

"When you're driving," I continued a little desperately, "you've got to keep your eyes up, at every intersection, for those stop signs . . ."

My old friend, looking very polite, said quietly:

"Thank you, very much, for explaining it to me."

And mad as a hornet, he drove off.

My starter went beezaweezaweeza, and was silent.

The Aristocrats

An old college chum of mine turned out to be an aristocrat, though of limited means. He was explaining to me the execrable bad manners of the motoring public.

"You see," he said, "the mass of mankind was never on wheels until the last two or three generations. Only people of means, the nobility and gentry, had the privilege of being carried. Mankind, you might say, has been pedestrian for thousands of years. And they don't know how to behave when they become buoyant or portable. The trouble with motor traffic today is that it suffers from delusions of grandeur. All kinds of red-necked peasants are getting carried away by their sense of importance. . . ."

I was driving him home, since he has no car. And I was able to point out to him a curious thing. The only rude drivers we encountered, as we bucked our way along the jammed and crowded thoroughfares, were people of obvious opulence and distinction. The only ones who blared their horns at us to get the heck out of the way were fine, iron-grey executive types of noble mien. The only ones who chivvied us out of line or rabbit-jumped us on the intersections were occupants of higher priced cars, with unquestionably lordly mien.

The only guy who stopped and waved us across a crowded cross-street was a homely looking cuss who looked as if he had a lunch pail in his beat up old car.

"Sir," I said to my old college chum, "I think the nobility and gentry are as mean as ever."

The Keys

Gil Purcell, general manager of Canadian Press, that organization for gathering and distributing news to which Canadian daily newspapers belong, is probably known to more Canadian newsmen of all levels than any other man in the business. And they are all fond of him for a number of reasons. But they respect him for his dynamic sense of action. He can make a decision as fast as any man, but can also make slow ones, which is highly important. As a rule, when he does a thing, it is done.

For example, while out for the evening with his wife, Gil lost his car key. The car was locked. The spare key was skilfully secreted inside the locked car. Such a thing should not happen to Purcell. The ensuing shemozzle sent out shock waves felt by his family and by midnight garages until Purcell got into his car.

The following morning, he bought six new car keys. He distributed them as follows: one at home, one in his wife's purse, one at the office, one secreted on the outside of his car, an extra one on a separate key ring on his person, and finally one screwed into his artificial leg. In the war, Gil lost his leg by being hit by a container of rations dropped from an infantry-supporting aircraft. That in itself is characteristic of Purcell, for the average Joe fated to lose a leg would have lost it in some humdrum fashion.

The thigh joint of the artificial limb is wooden and hollow. It is perfect for concealing a spare key, a fact that Purcell realized with considerable satisfaction, because he has felt for years that the possibilities of the leg were not being fully explored. He had the technicians fasten the key with a screw.

And it may safely be said that Purcell will not be locked out of his car again. If he remembers to carry a screwdriver.

Drag Race

In the five o'clock homing traffic, a car pulled past me going a good five, maybe ten miles per hour faster than the general flow of traffic. The driver of it, a square-built, prosperous gentleman of the aggressive school, cast me a frosty glance because a very small boy, who was a passenger in my jalopy, yelled at him irreverently.

Being a slow-lane type of driver, I rolled along with the herd until we came to a stop light. And before the light changed, I had drawn alongside the pushing, square-built gent. He glanced at me, and glanced away, bored by my continued presence. He thought he had left me behind, blocks ago.

As someone was turning left, and since he was in the centre, or faster-moving lane of traffic, I got away well ahead of him on the lights. And it was about three blocks before he overtook me, scooting hotly along at five or ten miles an hour faster than us slowpokes. My small boy passenger obliged by giving him a yell. He glanced and saw us again. A hint of annoyance was in his quickly averted face.

The next stop light, though you must take my word for it that I did no manoeuvring, I again drew level with the hustler, and the recognition was mutual. Once again, the cars ahead of him were slow on the breakaway, while my lane was nimble; and again it was three or four blocks before the efficient driver, as I have no doubt he felt himself to be, overtook and passed me. The small boy, this time with a little coaching, gave the proper hoot. Our adversary stepped on the gas and speeded up to fifteen miles an hour faster than the procession of all us dopes.

It was eight blocks to the next stop light. When we reached it, there was a small holdup. Our square-built executive was halted at the curb, and a policeman was standing at his open door, taking down various particulars.

"Hi!" yelled my small passenger, hearty and shrill.

I felt like pulling up and going back to apologize for the gentleman. After all, it was the fault of all us dopes that he was in trouble. If he hadn't looked upon us as dopes, he wouldn't have been going so fast.

The Shocker

The most cantankerous of my acquaintances is seldom happier than when driving his car in traffic. The more mixed up the traffic, the happier he becomes. He is completely surrounded by fools, and his cup is full. He blasts his horn. He steps on it. He brakes. His car jerks and shudders. He runs down the windows to glare and hurl imprecations. For two pins, he would get out of his car and punch somebody in the nose. A happy, cantankerous man.

One of his pet furies is against people who drive too close to his tail. He is always looking in the rear mirror to see if some fathead isn't practically bumping him. He gives some of them a bad moment by stamping on his brakes to scare them. It is, he says, the failure to keep a proper distance between cars that is the root of sixty per cent of all accidents. Until lately, it has grieved him that he had no way of expressing his feelings to these fools who crowd up on him.

Then he got the bright idea. If a horn in front is useful for correcting the faults of others, why not a horn in the rear, aimed backwards? So he had a fine, raucous, truck-type horn installed behind. And the astonishment of those motorists who come too close, when they get a blast in the face, is something to behold.

The Encumbrance

During the First World War there was a popular story about the recruiting sergeant who was having trouble interesting a prospect in the infantry. So he switched to the cavalry and pointed out the advantages of having a horse to ride. As a final pitch, he explained what a great thing a horse would be in case a retreat was ordered.

"In no retreat," said the prospect, "I don't want to have to drag no horse after me!"

Recently, I heard a group of young executives planning a visit to a downtown business conference.

"We'll go in my car," suggested one of them.

"No way," said another. "We don't want to have to drag a car around with us. We'll take a taxi."

In an ever-expanding area of business, especially in large cities, the personal motor car is becoming a nuisance, an encumbrance. It is no longer an efficient means of transportation. When you witness the woebegone parades of tens of thousands of cars grunting homeward, yard by yard, to the suburbs of the exploding metropoli, you are free to wonder how long the poor old gas buggy will be behind the horse and buggy in the history of the obsolete.

Progress

When I offered to drive a philosophic friend of mine to a meeting in a city a couple of hundred miles away to which we were both invited, he declined.

"Motoring is now," he said, "the most primitive form of transportation. Prior to the invention of the steam locomotive, the mass of mankind travelled entirely on foot, only the well-to-do and the farmers having horses or wagons. But now, at least hereabouts if not in India and China, the mass of mankind travels by motor car. Thus motoring has become primitive, tiresome, exhausting, nerve-racking. Motor cars push each other all over the place. Motoring is too costly, not only in money, both in capital investment and upkeep, but in nervous energy. Motoring a hundred miles is a bore. Motoring two hundred miles there and two hundred miles back is too primitive to contemplate."

"I suppose you will fly," I said.

"No, that is too primitive, too," he said. "It does not get you to your destination. It gets you only within an hour's primitive drive of your destination. Flying is in its infancy. No. I am going by train, the only entirely sure, effortless mode of transportation so far devised by man."

So I went by train too and a comfortable snooze was had by all.

The Haven

There is a superb calm about a railway ticket office. Amid the steadily mounting gale of our lives in this headlong era, a railway ticket office is like a cave beneath the waves. It has the curious sudden peace of a concrete bunker in an air raid.

Out of the clatter, clank and bang of the city you step into a stillness broken only by a slight shuffling. That's your feet, as you walk, slightly abashed, over to one of the line-ups at the wickets.

You join a queue. You peer over the shoulders ahead of you. There are a few muttered words.

The ticket agent has the telephone receiver cocked between his shoulder and his ear. Nothing moves. At the heads of the adjoining queues, customers, half way into the wickets, are muttering to other clerks.

The clerks move slowly. They reach back to racks and pick out pink or beige slips of paper and somberly pick up telephones to cock between shoulder and ear.

There they stand, entranced. Five clerks, with telephones cocked between shoulder and ear. They do not speak.

Nobody moves. Nobody speaks.

You are bewitched. You feel your blood starting to slow. Your pulse slackens. The tremors of the workaday subside. You sag.

And there the five clerks stand, motionless, the telephones cocked between shoulder and ear, hearing nothing.

The Horse Car

At the age of two, I was taken by my father for a ride on the last of the horse cars in Toronto. That was in 1894, when the last of the horse car routes, on McCaul Street, was withdrawn. Of course, I don't remember it. But in after years, my father told me that some day I would appreciate the fact that I had had a ride in a horse car.

Sure enough, I appreciated it a long time later while watching Col. Glen being shot into orbit. And as the hours passed during that fantastic and curiously classical, almost ceremonial, occasion, I could not help but reflect that there are not too many people left in the world who could be as astonished as I. It is the middle and younger generation who take the wonders of our time for granted.

My grandfather, who looked with misgivings on the electrification of the streetcars in those days, was credited with this:

"What do you expect to gain," he demanded, "by such extravagance? For what purpose did God put horses on earth?"

How long, long ago that was!

Home

When I was young and got home from the war, I said:

"Ah, how nice to be home."

When I was in my thirties, and the newspaper profession required me to be weeks and sometimes months abroad in the world in pursuit of some headline or other, there was nothing to compare with the sight of the suburbs of my native city from the train window.

"Ah, it's good to be home!"

In my fifties, I went hunting in the fall for ten days, or trout fishing in the spring for a week, and had a wonderful time, of course, but:

"Ah, it's good to be home!"

In December, my wife and I went downtown for three hours to do a little last minute shopping and to join for a little while in the bodily contact game of Christmas in the big stores. We made it. We got out of the milling doors of the great emporia. We clung together in the jammed bus. With high elbows, we fought our way to the bus exit and found we had reached the right stop.

"Ah," we said, making our escape in through our front door, "it's good to be home!"

Greetings Out Back

As far as I can find out, there is no law that can be invoked to make a property owner pull down a public eyesore. The most that can be done is to have the health authorities declare the premises unfit for human habitation or a menace to the public.

Thus in cities, towns and the countryside, all manner of decayed old houses, warehouses, sheds, barns and rickety structures of every description continue to offend the eye. This is particularly true of new super highways which, usually selecting routes that avoid the old established roads, cut across the backs of farms or go around the dilapidated edges of villages. Old tumbledown barns that have been out of sight of the former roads for fifty years now slant grey and drunken not fifty yards off the noble four lane. The back doors of shabby little farmhouses that were formerly concealed from everyone's view now open onto the transcontinental artery. Quite a few privies ornament the foreground.

And there isn't a thing that can be done about it.

Property is property. And maybe these eyesores are the expression of the dignity of property.

An elderly rural gentleman of my acquaintance has a privy that modestly faced away from his farmhouse but now faces a great speedway. It has always been his custom, over seventy years, to leave the door open. He still does.

"They wave at me," he says. "I wave at them."

84

Straight Furrows

Farmers still like to do their best plowing closest to the road. Over the hill, you may hear the tractor snorting at a great rate, and speed being made. You can catch glimpses of the farmer's head and shoulders as he jounces along towing his plows. But when he comes round near the road, in view of the passersby, he slows the tractor down.

And with what remains of that traditional pride farmers enjoyed as they handled their team of horses and the writhing plow handles in full view of the road the mechanized farmer steers his tractor at a reduced pace, turning his head constantly to see how the furrows roll. For a straight furrow remains the pride of a countryman.

Old farmers tell me that for all its hardship, spring plowing had a satisfaction about it that was unique. It was an art. The handling of a well-trained team of horses, the management of the plow itself, the constant attention upon everchanging character of the soil, even in a single field, all concentrated upon the one accomplishment, a perfect straight furrow—that was art. These old farmers declare there is as much difference between horse-plowing and tractor-plowing as there is between playing a piano and a mechanical piano.

But art is going out of industry, all over creation. Machines can do better than hands; machines add better than brains; the perfect machine is one in which its operator does not have to think at all.

Still, a million farmers think about having their best furrows nearest the road.

Winter Landscape

The man sitting beside me in the vista dome or blister of the trans-Canada train handed me the typewritten news bulletin which the porter had brought up to us, to be handed from passenger to passenger. Just the usual morning news bulletin on one sheet. I glanced over it and then tapped the passenger sitting ahead of me and handed it forward.

"Doesn't it make you sick?" asked my seat mate, a reserved, prosperous man.

"Same old stuff," I agreed. "War threats, riots."

"I have been sitting here," said the stranger, "looking at the farms as we go by. The farmhouses. Quiet in the snow. The barns. I guess you can see the roof of one farmhouse from the other."

"They look pretty snug." I said.

"These farmers," reflected the businessman, "must be a pretty happy people, now, as compared with the rest of us. They have peace. They have security. I mean, they have cattle, hogs, hens, barns full of feed. No matter what happens to the world, they know how to feed themselves and keep themselves warm, and they have the means to do it, the fields, gardens, woodlots, livestock."

We watched the quiet farms wheeling by. You could only count four or five farmhouses in any one glance over the landscape.

"What they have," said the stranger, "is privacy. That's it. That is the precious thing. The thing the missiles have destroyed, the satellites, all the processes of society have destroyed, is privacy. But look out there! Look at those quiet, aloof farms. Privacy!"

And in the city man's voice was a kind of desperation.

The Hint

Near the gate of a fairly lonely farm, I was puzzled to behold several large rocks, larger than bushel baskets, reposing balanced on top of the sturdy cedar fence posts.

They gave the impression of enormous mushrooms. How anybody could have the strength to hoist these walloping big round boulders up to the height of a fence post had me staggered. How patiently the man must have manoeuvred them and balanced them? And what purpose did they serve? Was it to hold the fence post down firmly in some weird elastic soil?

Being nosey by profession, I drove in the farm lane. A remarkably pretty young woman came out the side door of the farmhouse when I drew up. She was followed by another, younger and even prettier.

"Is the farmer in?" I requested, in the approved phraseology of that country.

"He's out back," the girls replied. And at that moment, an older woman, their mother, came to the door. She too was a most handsome woman. I confessed to her the sheer curiosity that had brought me up their lane, and the woman laughed.

"Aw, that's my husband's idea," she confided. "He put those stones up, years ago, when we were first married. It was meant as a warning to tramps and strangers to be polite to me if they came in. He wanted them to know a big strong man lived here."

We laughed, and I said I did not blame him in the least. The mother and I glanced appreciatively at the two lovely girls who were smiling quizzically, waiting.

"What's more," said the mother, "he has put up several new ones this last two or three years!"

The Labor Saver

We old-timers find it comical to listen to the rising generation bragging about their labor-saving devices. We had labor-saving devices fifty and seventy-five years ago that have these modern appliances and household gadgets beaten by miles. To see the modern young housewife dancing attendance on her batteries of washing machines, dryers, vacuum cleaners, automatic stoves, electric frying pans, electric can openers and all the rest, gives us the chuckles.

Our labor saving devices of bygone years had two legs. They were maids, and nearly every household had one. In villages and on farms, they were called "hired girls," and they cost $5 a month. They started operating, with no more than a $1 alarm clock, at 6 a.m. They cooked, they swept, they dusted, they scrubbed, they baked, preserved, washed, dried and ironed. They made beds. They ate in the kitchen, and sat there, in the evenings alone, until nine, when they crept up to their attic rooms.

They made life pretty comfortable for the lady of the house, fifty years ago, as comfortable as their brothers, fathers, sons and lovers made life for the gentleman of the house, down at the shop.

Mackenzie King's
Bad Luck

Mackenzie King once told me that he had tried two or three times to become interested in fishing, on the urging of friends. But on those few occasions he went fishing, they had no luck, and he had lost interest in it.

It is very important that you choose the time and the place, when attempting to convert a friend to angling. Every addict of the sport knows that there are plenty of blank days. These do not discourage him, but merely excite him all the more. If fishing were sure-fire, it would be as dull as visiting the fish store. But the beginner who has no luck is unaware of this. The beginner should always catch fish, and see plenty of fish being caught. Never take a possible convert on a trip that is doubtful.

If Mackenzie King's friends had borne this in mind, the whole course of the man's life might have been changed. The first thing that would have happened to him would have been marriage. You can't become an angler without visiting the homes of your companions, not in the parlor or living room, but right back in the kitchen, where the trout are laid out on the table. You even go upstairs to the attic or down to the cellar of your friend's homes to help carry out his tackle and gear. It is in such places, you meet the sisters of your companions in unpresentable condition, with their hair in curlers, and wearing old kimonos or sweaters. They might be even all flushed over pies or cakes in the oven. It is seeing girls in this condition that finishes a man. Even Mackenzie King, with all his caution, could hardly have withstood the charms of one of his angling companions' sisters washing the dishes. That is usually fatal.

But, no. Mackenzie King never caught a fish. No woman ever cut him down to size. No children bothered the life out of him. In solitary dedication, he pursued his way, all because his friends took him fishing on a dud day.

Lucked

You can have all the talent in the world but without luck you are, as the saying goes, out of luck. You take fishing, for example. I have devoted much of my life to becoming, in my own opinion at any rate, a very skilful and wise angler with various types of gear. Some years ago, I, in my cautious fashion, observed a very large muskie who inhabited a weed bed in about ten feet of water. I had a perfect view of him, and he was a trophy fish. In early dawn, in bright noon and in the cool of the evening, when the fishing begins, I went after that fish. With skill, with cunning, with every wile, I coaxed it with every lure I knew, save a dead sucker. It ignored me and all my skill.

One noon day, three boys in a noisy rowboat came past where I was sitting brooding on the shore. They were trolling an eight inch sucker on a coarse line as heavy as a clothes line.

They hooked and landed that muskie. It weighed thirty-two pounds.

They had luck. And am I right in assuming they had nothing else? Ah, that is a question.

The Disturbing Peace

There is an insatiable human instinct to disturb the peace. Up at the cottage, the lake was still as a millpond and a lovely autumn mist hung over it. A flock of some thirty wild geese came in and landed well out in the middle. Not three minutes elapsed before a grown man jumped in his outboard and raced full pelt out, for what purpose it would be hard to say, since shooting was not yet open on that water. The geese took off before he was half way to them, and vanished.

There he careened and scooted around in silly circles, kicking up swells in the quiet water; and then came tamely back to his wharf. When some of us wandered over and enquired in a nice way what the Sam Hill he meant by this exhibition, he appeared genuinely puzzled.

"It just seemed like a good idea," he said.

It seems like a good idea to a young man, for instance, to install an exponential muffler on his mini car, and go snorting and thundering through quiet residential streets at 2 a.m.

The peace and quiet of the schoolroom are unbearable both to small boys and girls alike, so when they get out at recess it is necessary to scream and yell and race wildly about. Peace and quiet, you might say, anywhere, are insufferable to the natural young. They must whoop and holler, kick over ash cans, hammer on fences, run, jump, wrestle, stamp.

No man is happier than one with a power shovel. And all other men pause and envy him.

An old friend of mine with thirty years as a streetcar motorman has been promoted to the subway trains.

"All I can do," he says wistfully, "is blow the silly little tin whistle."

With his mouth. For years, he had a great bell to clang with his foot.

Peace is not natural to man. To feel alive, he must disturb it.

The Splash

For good or ill, men have almost entirely abandoned walking sticks. The popular attitude towards sticks is scornful. A very aged lady was attempting to cross an icy intersection. She carried a cane with a rubber cap on its end. To reach the curb, she had to take a long step across a puddle of slush: and there she teetered, trying to get a good bite on the pavement with her stick. Being at heart a Boy Scout, I came to her aid and helped her to terra firma, whereupon I showed her the steel spike I carry on the tip of my cane. While we were conversing, another lady of middle age, all dressed up in that afternoon style peculiar to ladies who belong to busy women's organizations, slipped on the same icy hummock and then came down a slosher in the puddle of slush almost at our feet. I never saw a lady take a more complete fall into a puddle. She lay there, sprawled not in pain but in fury that this should have happened to her. The aged lady and I assisted her, not without a good deal more of sprawling and slithering, to her feet. As we assisted in wiping her off, I assured her, indicating my stick as well as the aged lady's, that she might well carry a cane in such weather. She withered me with a glance.

"Do you think I want to look ridiculous?" snorted the very ridiculous lady.

Thumb Stick

In Scotland and the north of England, the thumb stick has been popular for generations. For walking in the country, a thumb stick is every bit as comforting as sturdy old boots.

In length, it should just reach your armpit, from the ground. Its top consists of a simple crotch, the smaller the better, for your thumb to fit over. A good straight thumb stick is a hard thing to find. The gypsies, who search out and cut most of the walking sticks for the trade in the British Isles, keep their eyes peeled for beautiful specimens of the crotched thumb stick in blackthorn, holly and various other woods that are light and strong. For they get good prices for them from men like Ben Cox, whose stick shop, opposite Selfridge's in Oxford Street, is one of the most famous in the world.

When walking with a thumb stick, you grasp it about ten inches or so from the crotch and use it like a light staff as you stride along. But when you come to a hill or slope, the thumb stick becomes a miraculous thing, like an extra leg. You shift your grip up to the top, setting your thumb in the crotch. And with the stick slanted back, you go up hill like a feather. The Scottish shepherds use them more commonly than crooks. Men like the late Lord Tweedsmuir made collections of them. In Canada, they are becoming popular amongst trout fishermen on the trails in the back country. They are every bit as good as your second wind on a portage.

Hunting for thumb sticks in the woods is a fascinating hobby. Maple and oak offer the most crotches, but are often too thick to make good sticks. They should be a little thicker than your middle finger. Such woods as ash, ironwood, elm, have the best quality, but you can hunt for hours without getting a proper crotch on a straight stick.

But hunting for sticks slows you down, in the woods. You take your time. Your eyes are everywhere. With the result that you see about ten times as much of the animal and plant life of the woods as you would notice on an ordinary walk.

Thinking Bach

We are so flooded, bombarded, smothered by entertainment from all directions that we are left little opportunity to entertain ourselves. TV, radio, Hi-Fi, movies, sport, the newspapers, magazines. Go into a restaurant, and what do you find besides something to eat? Entertainment. The streets have striven to be entertaining for centuries. But now they are turning streets into malls. It looks as if we are being entertained to death.

Okay. How do I entertain myself?

By thinking about Bach and Mozart. If they had, in their wildest dreams, ever imagined the hundreds of millions of people who would one day be listening to their work all over the earth, what would they do? I think they would have suffered stage fright and panicked.

For the world in which they worked was a small world. Music, except squeeze boxes, fiddles in villages, wheezy organs in town churches, was largely confined to the cities. Even in cities, the musical world revolved around the courts of small kings and petty dukes who employed musicians as they would chefs. And the musicians flocked together and wrote compositions for one another as much as for anybody else.

Confining my reading to fishing tackle catalogues and that sort of thing, I have never read a biography of Mozart or any other great musician. But when you are tempted to quit a golf game in order to hustle home and catch a certain program on TV, read a biography of Mozart instead of going golfing. It will entertain you with the idea that we are being entertained to death.

Mad Thought

A quiet lady of my acquaintance was reading a program for the public observance of Remembrance Day. When she came to the brief line in the list of ceremonies referring to the one minute of silence, she remarked:

"What we should have, all over the earth, is one day of silence. A universal day of silence during which no one speaks. And everybody thinks."

A day of stillness. No newspapers, no radio or TV. No cars moving on the streets. No factories working, no stores open, no policemen directing traffic. No deliveries. No stoves cooking. No taps running.

Stillness, all over the earth, and nothing on earth to do but think.

It would be unbearable. We could not face it. Half the world would go mad, and the rest would be dissolved in tears.

For fear of thinking, we have devised a world full of a thousand distractions.

The Unviewers

My family is thinking of getting rid of our TV set, all on my account. This is not due to my addiction to it, to the neglect of my work. The reverse is the case. I disregard the TV shamefully, spending my evenings unsociably up in my den until such time as I hear a scream or a pistol shot down in the living room.

Whereupon, I lay my book down and descend to the living room and join my family circle. They are knitting, or playing cards, or else just chatting casually while, on the TV bright amidst them, a thrilling drama is being enacted.

"Who," I interrupt them, "fired the shot? Who is that lying dead over there in the corner? What's the girl doing with the gun in her hand? What's it all about . . .?"

I am turned upon indignantly by one and all.

"If you want to watch the TV," they declare, "move it up to your den. Nobody's watching it here."

Then what was it on for?

Nobody knows. Nobody noticed it was on.

Foul-Weather Friends

During a period of sloppy weather, I was able to make a most interesting survey. And the net result is that it is the nicest, gentlest, sweetest people who track mud and slush into your house.

The hardboiled stinkers, the cold, ruthless, crafty-eyed self-centred characters whom you admit in the front door with the greatest reluctance are the ones who invariably take off their rubbers or galoshes outside the front door and step into your living room with dry shoes. If they haven't rubbers on, it is these unlovable, hard-boiled, disagreeable acquaintances whose arrival at your door always fills you with an indescribable dismay who carefully wipe their feet on the mat outside, and tip-toe in with careful backward glances to make sure they are not leaving any tracks behind them.

But when you greet some dear old friend, some sweet, heart-warming, most welcome guest at your door, what does she or he do?

In they tramp with a pound of slush on each foot. With the greatest innocence, they bulge joyously into your living room with its pale green broadloom, wall to wall, and leave gobbets of mud with every pace.

Seat them in the chair of the guest of honor, and from their insteps drip, minute by minute, gobs of muck to create darkening pools under each foot.

What is it about the nicest people that they always have slush on their feet?

Who's There

Telephone manners have always been good, on the whole. Almost from the beginning of the telephone, we adopted a very simple routine. When the bell rings, we pick up the implement and say "Hello." Who selected this greeting from among all the things we might have chosen will forever remain a mystery. In England they pick up the thing and say "Are you there?" In France, they cry "Allo!" to greet you, and then say "Allo?" with a question mark. It is very stylish. In Russia, I am informed, it is usually the wrong number, so you pick the phone up when it rings and growl: "Who will you be wanting this time, tovarish?"

In recent years, in business circles, the fashion is to lift the receiver when the bell rings and bark your name into it. "Bmmffssh here!" you bark, very alert. You are quite often the wrong guy. Another snappy trick is to say "Yess?" rather sharply. That is the popular mode of answering the phone in smart ladies' wear shoppes.

On the only occasion on which I ever got Winston Churchill on the telephone, it was by mistake. I was merely trying to get his fifth assistant secretary. The great man lifted the receiver (one of those clicketty-bonk English telephone receivers) and he greeted me as follows:

"Mmmmmmm?"

Maybe he was reading some important despatch, his mind absent. Maybe his cigar had got stuck to his lip. Possibly I had interrupted him having a snooze. But there it was, the unmistakable, the inimitable Churchill, even in uttering "Mmmmmmm?"

"I beg your pardon," I whispered, and hung up and took a bus over to Whitehall where, being unable to see the assistant fifth secretary, I got him on the phone from the porter's desk downstairs. The porter got him on the line for me.

Callers

If your friends don't telephone you as often as you think they should, maybe it is because they can't get you off the phone, once they do call.

The psychology of telephoning is this: if you call some one, it is up to you to terminate the conversation, in the thought that the other person may be busy or interrupted in some task. The person called always has the excuse to say, well, I guess I'll have to go, dear, I've got something on the stove. But if someone calls you, you assume they have time on their hands or they wouldn't have called. And you can therefore go on and on and on. . . .

And many people do go on and on. I have two friends, one a man and one a woman, whom I never call on the phone because it means up to half an hour before I can disentangle their clutches. Over the years I have worked out a whole battery of excuses with which I can break off when they call me. Sometimes, I am expecting a long distance call I've put in. Or, oh, there's the door bell. Maybe I'm sorry, but I've got a chap here visiting me on business. That's a good one. My friends can visualize the poor fellow sitting there, while I'm tied onto the phone.

Mind you, it isn't as if I don't see these two friends frequently. Indeed, I usually see them once or twice every week. But there seems to be something cosy and confidential about the telephone. They can think up things to say that never occur to them when you are face to face. And relax. My woman friend has an extension phone up in her bedroom, and she prefers to call me about 2 p.m. I can see her, after a nice, comfortable lunch, reclining on her bed, her cigarettes handy, the telephone not necessarily even held in her hand, but resting by her ear on the pillow, while she indulges in a long, lazy chat with me, or whoever else is on her list.

So now I set the alarm on my small desk clock whenever she calls, and after five minutes, I twist the setter, the alarm rings sharply. It's a dandy idea. She doesn't know what it's all about. All I have to do is exclaim hastily: "I've got to go!"

And I do.

The Courtesy Grabbers

After a train trip and a sojourn in hotels for three days, I have the impression that the ladies who have the least right to courtesy are those who expect it the most. Despite the tremendous changes in feminine character during the past generation, there still remain a fair number of the sex that have preserved a domineering and haughty bearing as the hallmark, they suppose, of the lady of quality. Back in the days of the drama of Oscar Wilde and Arthur Wing Pinero, it was known as the grand manner, and whole sections of our Canadian community, known as Society, practiced it. Young ladies' finishing schools were devoted to teaching the art of the brush-off for all lesser breeds without the law. You could be sweet, but it had to be a lofty sort of sweetness. The milkman, the store clerk, the man who shovelled the snow, were expected to quail before it.

By now, of course, the lofty manner should be deader than ostrich fans. But it isn't. And if you keep an eye skinned you can still see it. I opened a car door on my way to the dining car. Three ladies of mature years, but still nimble, were just rounding the corridor. They swept through, as I held the door, with the lofty air and never a word, much less a glance of thanks, as they warbled past, employing the throaty voice of what, in the TV movies of the 1930 vintage is represented as the cultured tone of the better class. In the hotel elevator, one of these antique dames, though only about forty, swept in and instructed the operator to take her up at once, as she did not like to be in a crowded elevator. The poor kid, flabbergasted, did.

At the hotel cigar counter, I had just bought a packet of cigarettes, which was lying on the counter while I groped for my money. A lofty lady in the clothes of, say, an executive's wife, picked up my packet, dropped some coins and said:

"I'm rather in a hurry."

Courtesy still survives for the ladies, though; but only for those who don't demand it.

Characters

An office building which I frequently have to enter is growing a little out of date. It has reached the stage that it seems always to need paint, and there is a frowsy sort of newsstand in its lobby. It has three elevators, only two of which are normally running.

The elevator operators are middle-aged men, maybe a trifle worse than middle-aged. Sometimes they are in full uniform, which is grey with tired silver braid around the lapel edges. Sometimes they are in half uniform, and at other times they turn up in any old clothes.

And they are the worst-tempered old coots you ever met.

"Come on, come on!" they will snarl at the passengers to hurry them aboard.

They slam the doors in your face just as you are stretching out to enter. Their answers to enquiries from passengers are in grunts and mutters. They never look at anyone. Something else is always on their minds. They engage in hostile badinage with the newsstand girl and with the rowdy office boys who are always congregated in the lobby drinking cokes.

They are surly, insolent, impolite and full of growls.

The general manager of the company that owns the building and occupies two floors of it is an old acquaintance of mine.

"It's time," I said to him, when I just about had my nose clipped off by rudely slammed elevator gates. "It's time you fired or pensioned off those two rheumatic old Airedales you've got running your elevators."

"Who?" cried my friend, astonished. "You mean Herbie and Joe?"

"I never felt attracted to learning their names," I admitted. "But they're impossible."

"Why," expostulated my friend, "they're characters!"

"Characters, is it?" I reflected.

And I reflected further on the thought that a great many ill-mannered, grumpy, crotchety people, both sexes, get away with murder among their familiars, being promoted to characters.

Jammed

As a permanent resident in a large hotel, I see a great variety of human kind, both local and from foreign parts. And the most amusing feature of life is the attitude of the guests and the public towards elevators.

There is a battery of six elevators in this hotel. They are automatic, operated with buttons by the passengers. They perform with astonishing regularity. I have seldom been kept waiting thirty seconds for an elevator, and rarely sixty seconds. There are frequently two or three of them empty and waiting at the main floor lobby.

But you would think every elevator is the last one on earth. The guests rush and crowd into one car, even when there are two others standing open. There is an anxiety and urgency about their behavior that is hard to understand. What's the hurry?

Compared with only twenty years ago, when I was inhabiting hotels all over America and Europe, this anxiety is truly a social phenomenon. As recently as the nineteen forties, when there was ample justification for a good deal of anxiety and hurry, people in hotels, department stores and office buildings, were patient, usually courteous and polite. They did not storm the elevators. The sense of being jammed is being boiled into us. Maybe we are a jammed society.

The Heckler

At a reception for a great Canadian industrialist, men and women of all levels of the community were invited including such lowly characters as newspapermen. I was standing fairly close to the guest of honor, sampling the exchanges of conversation between him and the diverse types he had to tilt wits with. On the fringe of the crowd around him was one old codger, a tall, lean, grey-haired man who was obviously busting to come to grips with the tycoon. He was one of that type you see at political meetings who is always heckling, getting to his feet time and again, and prepared, if necessary, to make a speech himself. Big nosed, fiery-eyed, head thrown back—the argumentative windbag species known to every reporter everywhere.

Finally he edged his way in, held his hand out heartily, seized the poor tycoon's in a wrestler's grasp, and said, loudly, rudely and provocatively:

"Well, I guess you figure you're the biggest toad in the puddle, now, eh? All I want to say . . ."

Somebody rescued the guest of honor by lunging in and greeting him effusively, shouldering the crank to one side. And in the crowd he never got another crack at his victim, whatever it was he had to say.

But in the following half hour, I happened upon the old windbag three separate times in three separate locations in the big reception room. In each instance, he was regaling a small group with an account of what he had said to the great man, with the easy and knowing air of one who speaks his mind, even to the big shots. When I got my coat and hat and was leaving the hotel, who should I see talking to the doorman, and pulling on his gloves in the best Micawber style, but my old friend the windbag. As I passed, I heard him tell the doorman, humorously, offhandedly, as one man of the world to another:

"Do you know what I said to him? If the people you took your money off were laid end to end . . ."

Goodness knows what his story would be by the time he got home to tell his wife and the boarders. He is a type from whom no prime minister, no president of a bank or a hockey club, no man of position anywhere is safe. In our democratic system, the heckler is part of the arrangement.

106

Help

"The guest is always right," used to be the slogan of the hotel business. In a hotel, I wanted my room made up early because I had to interview some people and had invited them to the hotel for this purpose. On my way to breakfast, I spoke to the two maids I encountered in the corridor, shoving their housekeeping pram from room to room.

I told them my room number and phrased my request as pleasantly as possible. They looked at me and grunted and went on folding towels.

When I returned to my room, it was just as I had left it, bed rumpled, ash trays loaded, newspapers on the floor. My guests were due in half an hour. I telephoned the manager.

"You realize how help is, these days," he said sadly, and put me in touch with the floor housekeeper.

A weary lady in black came to my room and I explained to her what I had done, how I had spoken to the maids, hung the card on my door, in accordance with the printed instructions.

"Well, you know how help is, nowadays," replied the housekeeper, helplessly.

In the same hotel, I boarded an elevator and sang out my floor. When I was carried past the floor and protested, the operator assured me:

"You gotta speak up!"

At lunch, a very stately, lovely young lady led me to a table, smilingly handed me the menu and, smiling and stately, walked away. An extremely cranky and hurried waitress came and furiously dusted off the tablecloth, poised her pad whilst gazing elsewhere.

"What'll it be?" she demanded, definitely impatient.

I ordered. She brought me the wrong thing and was most indignant with me for it being wrong.

In our democratic determination to uphold the dignity of the human individual, we are discovering that human dignity clothes some surliness, considerable sloppiness and quite a bundle of self-righteousness.

Impedimenta

With all the talk about H-bombs and mass destruction, I found myself starting to pack, as it were.

Of all the worldly goods with which a man endows himself, what would he take if, suddenly, in the middle of the night, he had to leave all and head for the open country or the wilderness?

If he had his car, what would he take along? Tables,

chairs? No. Pictures, paintings? No. Cutlery? Yes; the practical kind. Dishes? No; only a few pots and pans that would easily go into the car trunk.

Books? Ah! That is a tough one. You can stand in front of your few hundred books and try to figure which dozen or twenty of them you would dare give precious space to in your car, if heading, desperately and without delay, into the unknown. Allow yourself only twelve books, and see for yourself which you would take.

Blankets, ah yes! Clothes? Only the warmest, roughest, most durable. Boots, socks, leather windbreakers, rain coats. Mitts rather than gloves. Sweaters rather than shirts. It is astonishing how little of what a man's house is filled with would be useful in case of the great emergency that now fills the minds of premiers, presidents, scientists. It is staggering to think how much of our earthly possessions we would abandon without a second thought.

But suppose we could not take the car. Suppose we had to take only what we could carry on our backs and in valises in our hands.

We certainly could not take twelve books. Could we take three? And what three would they be, out of all these hundreds . . .?

And which coat, which boots, which knives from the kitchen drawer, not the dining room drawer. Which pots, which pans? A little exercise of the mind in this direction invests with a startling dignity the homeliest articles in your house.

Everybody's English

No wonder English is becoming the language of the world. As the British Empire has dwindled before our eyes, the English language has flourished like anything you care to compare it to, depending on your prejudices.

The reason for its popularity is that it is lawless. There must be some law that states that the more lawless a thing is, the more popular it is. French, German, the classic languages, are all corsetted in tight-fitting laws. But English is wild, free, piratical. Anybody can talk it, though reading and writing it is something a little more difficult.

Take that comic series known to all newcomers to English-speaking countries, the "through" syndrome. Through, cough, dough, plough, enough, on and on go the oughs. And practically all have a different sound.

What they call the King's English is a myth. I suppose the inventor of the term meant English as it is taught at Oxford, for example. A large proportion of the students at the Oxford colleges, I am told, are sent by their families to learn the accent, nothing much more. If you have the accent, you are in. But from one end of England to the other, not mentioning Scotland and Ireland, you will hear English spoken in forty ways. And in Canada, the United States, Australia, India and elsewhere, they have their regional dialects.

Yet we all understand one another.

With mutual pleasure.

Waw Cry

On the TV news a member of an English delegation at Geneva was being interviewed on the day's proceedings.

"As Sir Winston Churchill once said," remarked this gentleman, "jor, jor, jor is better than waw, waw, waw."

Now, I beg to differ. Sir Winston said nothing of the kind. What he said, quite clearly, was:

"Jaw, jaw, jaw is better than waw, waw, waw."

And that makes sense.

When we say it in Canadian, it comes out:

"Jaw, jaw, jaw, is better than war, war, war."

It loses almost as much punch in Canadian as it does in that particular brand of English the gentleman employs who calls it "jor, jor, jor."

For real euphony, we might combine the two, and make it:

"Jor, jor, jor is better than war, war, war."

But that is absurd too.

So what we had better all do is just leave it entirely to Sir Winston; and if we can't capture his own inimitable way of saying it, let us carry it as a tender echo in our memories and never try to repeat it at all.

Jeckdoes

On the TV I heard one of our Canadian actresses referring to a jeckdoe.

I know she is a Canadian actress, because I know her aunt, and have been in the village where she was born.

But she has fallen in with a curious company of Canadians who have studied and adopted a most tiddly, fiddly, diddly sort of English pronunciation.

This jeckdoe, for instance. Jeckdoe. It sounds like an animal. Maybe a bird. Maybe an Australian marsupial. I listened intently, parting my way, as it were, through the rushes and reeds of her pronunciation. Jeckdoe, there it was again! And then I got it. For it appears the jeckdoes were

112

flying around the spah of this old church which was involved in the drama.

Jackdaws, that's what they were! And the spah of the church was its spire.

Now, I know the argument about what is and what is not English is likely never to be settled. You can put a Scot from Glasgow, a Scot from Inverness, an Englishman from Yorkshire, another from Durham, another from Devon and three from London, itself, one from dahn arahnd Shoreditch, another from Threadneedle Street and still another from New Bond Street, (up it a little way!) all in one room. And then ask: what is the proper pronunciation of English?

Are none of these in the room proper? Who is to determine propriety? Oxford? Sir Laurence Olivier? The schoolmaster at BBC who instructs all those boys to emit their curious apothecary announcements in pure little glass nubbins, sterilized?

But as for our Canadian actors and actresses, how can we protect them from seeing jeckdoes? Should they not at all costs preserve the speech with which they were born, perfecting it, 'tis true, in all respects save altering its authentic sounds. There is a way to say jackdaw in Canada that cannot be improved upon: indeed, it is the way Olivier says it.

Maybe if we got into the habit of referring to those who, male or female, fall for the affected accent as jeckdoes, it might arrest the trend. Say the word out loud yourself, now, and hear how silly it sounds.

Pudaytas Inna Bag

The lady ahead of me in the cashier's line-up in the supermarket was well dressed, smart, bright. She certainly did not look as if she had quit school in grade seven.

"Can you," she asked the cashier, "put the pudaytas in a separate bag, please?"

"Sernly, ma'am," said the cashier.

And she put the pudaytas in a separate bag.

"Would you pahfer a cart'n," asked the cashier, "insteada a bag for the resta the stuff?"

"Thad be nice," agreed the lady. "Howja arrange to get sumbuddy to kerry the stuff out-ta ma car?"

"I'll buzz fer a boy ma'am," said the cashier. "It'll oney be a minnitt."

A tall youth came. He never opened his mouth. So my lesson in Canadian dialect came to an end.

There definitely is growing a Canadian dialect. It is as distinct from English and American dialects as they are from each other. The Canadian dialect consists first of all of elision. Vowels are dropped wherever possible. Nobody says Ham-il-ton anymore. They pronounce it Ham'l't'n. It comes close to being one syllable, instead of three. Not a bark or snort, exactly, but a sound that might be made if the mouth were full of warm pancake with maple syrup.

The letter T is changed to D whenever possible, as in pudayta, bedder for better, vederan, moder-car, hod-dog, wader for waiter and dozens of others you can hear all around you in the next half hour, if you listen.

We elide, we soften, we choose the laziest sound offered. We drop our G's. I ought to know. A lady called me on the phone.

"I heard you," she said, "on the air last night. I am a school teacher. I try to teach my children how to enunciate English. You referred to the Arctic as the Artick, and you dropped more than sixty per cent of your G's."

Gee!

Dynamite

In the north country I had dinner with a district judge, who has occasionally to sit in judgment while his conscience pricks him like a pin left in a new shirt. Quite a number of the cases that come before him have to do with backwoodsmen and gallant toilers on the frontier who have committed some crime associated with the forest or the stream. Lately he had to deal with two men who were found in possession of a quantity of dynamite, and they could offer the police no reasonable excuse for its possession.

When the dynamite was mentioned before the court, the judge says he began to prickle all over, as with the itch. It was his conscience.

"For I remembered," he said, "as though it were yesterday, being a young man on a survey party up here in this same country. And the man in charge of our party was a really great engineer, as time proved. But he was also fond of fish. And one evening, he mildly suggested that we chuck a stick of dynamite into a little lake we were camped on. He had come by a stick from a construction engineer on a railway job.

"All of us knew it was strictly illegal. But here we were, deep in the wilds, with nobody within twenty miles of us. Being the youngest of the party, and with not the slightest suspicion that I would one day become a judge, I think my conscience was the least disturbed of all. The boss rigged the dynamite up in a lard ball, and I was one of the two youths who paddled him out to the chosen spot. The bomb was dropped in the water, and we paddled furiously out of danger.

"The explosion went off. Maybe a dozen medium sized fish rose stunned to the surface. Now, before that bomb exploded, there may have been one gull sitting on a rock nearby. But before we could paddle the short distance to our loot, fifteen gulls appeared as if by magic and got every last fish. We arrived to find a couple of soggy looking suckers for our pains.

"Many a time, as I sit on the bench, I see gulls, ghostly gulls, flying about my court room."

The Secret

There is only one thing worse than having to keep a secret. And that is forgetting what the Sam Hill the secret was.

On our return to our cottage from a visit to one of our kinfolk, my son and I were preparing to retire and put out the lamp.

"By the way," said my son, his hand on the little wheel that turns down the wick, "what was that thing we weren't supposed to mention?"

"What thing?" I enquired.

"Don't you remember? We were let in, very confidentially, on something. A secret that we weren't supposed to breathe to a soul."

"Oh, yeah," I agreed. "Now what was it?"

We paused and struggled with memory. But it wouldn't come back.

My son blew out the lamp and silence descended on the cabin. I was unable to come to grips with sleep. What in blazes was that secret we had been let in on? Inch by inch, I went over the details of the evening at the family gathering.

"Hey!" hissed my son. "Have you thought of it yet?"

Finally we fell asleep. And we have never remembered what we were instructed to forget.

Most frustrating.

A.Y.

Lawren Harris and A. Y. Jackson, two of Canada's greatest artists, were on a sketching expedition in the northern wilderness. They came to a lake where Jackson immediately found a view that suited him. A great cedar had fallen into the water, its outer end curving up several feet above the water, providing a perfect seat where the artist could set up his sketch block amid the branches. Lawren Harris decided to push on farther up the shore, but would return in plenty of time to walk back to their camp.

Jackson perched in the fallen tree, far over the water, for the usual four or more hours, making his sketch of the landscape spread before him.

Presently he heard the sound of what he presumed to be Harris returning. The rustling and crashing in the brush continued right up to the shore end of the great tree suspended over the water.

"Have any luck?" enquired Jackson, over his shoulder, going on painting. He was a brief talking man.

No answer.

"See anything that suited you?" repeated Jackson, louder, but still not turning. No artist cares to waste a moment of light.

No answer.

Jackson heard his friend starting to come out on the leaning trunk.

"Get anything worth while?" enquired Jackson, volubly, for him.

Still no answer.

So Jackson twisted around on his precarious perch. And there, twenty feet away, on the fallen tree over the water, stood a large bear.

"Hello!" said Jackson.

The bear reared up on his hind legs and twisted an astonished nose in the air. Then it hastily wheeled and hurried off into the bush, reflecting, doubtless, on the incredible things one can find in trees.

Iris

Over the telephone, a commanding male voice demanded: "Iris there?"

There is no Iris in our household. In fact, I don't believe we know any girl named Iris.

"Just a moment, please," I said, setting the receiver down and going ahead with my reading.

After I read part of the page, I picked the phone up and said:

"Just a moment."

Then I got up and put the kettle on. I got out the tea pot, the tea and a cup and saucer.

To lend a little romance to the situation, I called clearly, for the benefit of the gruff gent waiting on the phone:

"Iris! Oh, Iris!"

Going over to the phone, I said:

"I'll see if I can get her."

An impatient snort came from the receiver.

I went out to the veranda and looked up and down. I went back in and tiddled the tea kettle on the burner.

"Iris!" I yodelled, musically. "I-ris!"

And then, having kept the gent a good minute longer, I went and took the receiver.

"I'm afraid," I said meekly, "you must have the wrong number. There is no Iris here."

The clunk with which the gentleman slammed down his receiver was a pleasure to hear. I hope he cracked it.

For the people who get wrong numbers deserve no sympathy. It is true this gentleman in quest of Iris did not much disturb me. I was only reading. But suppose I had been asleep? Or in a dark room developing films? Or half way up a column of figures I was trying to add? Anyway, from the sound of his voice, I feel sorry for Iris, and am glad I kept her free of him if only for a minute.

The Trouble With Water

One of my relations has newly bought a sloop, a small sailing craft. This has caused great interest and excitement among our circle of family and friends. It is without reservation of any kind that I confess that the whole thing leaves me cold. If there is any experience more exhausting than sitting in a small boat going no place in particular and with no thought in mind but going gurgly-slap-gurgle bump over miles of empty water, you name it.

My trouble, I suppose, is a form of claustrophobia. I feel a helpless and suffocating sense of isolation on a sail boat that is merely sailing. All around is nothing but water, surely the least interesting of the elements unless there are fish in it, and you after them. Just water, all the same color, all the same shape. Now and again, a gull comes wandering by, with that sense of hopelessness characteristic of gulls. One gull is much the same as any other gull.

And every minute, the land, blessed land, full of a thousand, a million interests in every nook and cranny of it, no two aspects of it the same, draws farther and farther away.

I do not expect to be invited on the new sloop.

Mystery Writers

I have had occasion to receive a great many letters from old friends. And it is perfectly astonishing how many of them are signed by totally undecipherable signatures. With the help of the phone book, I have been able to sleuth the identity of my friends by guessing, and then looking up the addresses. But that is only for the in-town ones. By poking through the waste basket and finding and matching up envelopes, I have succeeded in identifying other dear old buddies whose letters were entirely legible, but whose signatures were hieroglyphics like unto Egypt's. One that has me beaten appears to be a W followed by a wavy line three inches long. Another mystery looks like Screwdriver, but I am jiggered if I can recollect a Screwdriver among my old acquaintances. There is an Olphrap, a Weefis and a wonderful, tender, kindly old friend who appears to be Noofn.

I suppose after fifty or a hundred years, a man gets a little tired of writing his name on countless cheques, letters, contracts, receipts and all the other things that encompass us in the new documentary world.

But it seems to me there ought to be a law.

Couples

Much of the fun on a motor trip lies in observing your fellow travellers. When you pull up for lunch at some small town you never heard of before, it becomes a game to try and pick out the fellow travellers from the natives who are sitting around you in the restaurant. In Omaha, which are the Omahans and which the pilgrim from Vermont or Saskatchewan? You become fairly expert in the realization that you are as often wrong as right.

When two couples, travel-tanned and with that look of having just got out of a car, come in to sit at a table for four, you know you have a party of fellow travellers.

After speculating as to where they come from, the next question is: how are they paired off? Which woman is married to which man, in the four. Sometimes husband and wife sit opposite each other. Sometimes they sit side to side on the corners. There is no rule to help you here.

It was my wife who explained to me how to pair off the parties of four correctly.

"When one of the men," she said, "makes a witty remark and one of the women laughs, she's the wife of the other fellow."

A little research proves this to be a reliable guide.

The Old Postman

An old retired postman of my acquaintance, letter carriers they are called nowadays, telephoned me to bring him up some of my fine guinea fowl feathers, dyed a lovely pale bronze color, which I got from Scotland, and with which are tied a particular trout fly entitled in my honor the Sneaky. My old friend amuses himself in the winters tying flies.

He was in bed when I arrived. It was a notably foul day, with sleet, wild wind and rain flying horizontally. When I came into the sunroom where he lay, I immediately expressed my sympathy.

"Heck," said the old postman, "I never felt better. But I always stay in bed in weather like this. I just love to lie here by the hour looking out the window at the rain and the sleet. I love to hear the rain lashing the window glass. I leave that window slightly ajar so the wind will moan and whistle. And I just lie here, thinking of all the thirty-five years I spent, six days a week, winter, summer, spring, fall, carrying a great big bag of mail and walking my route."

"And thinking," I added, "of all the tens of thousands of people right now who are out in it."

"Oh," he said, "nothing is better than a blizzard, and I get up at break of day to sit at my window and watch the poor creatures wading through it."

The old postman's payoff, we can call it.

The Piper

Every little orchestra you see on TV or in the nightclubs has a bull fiddle in it. In symphony orchestras, I have seen six or eight of the massive instruments banked against the back wall, tremendously sounding out the beat as their masters bend and saw. The question now before us is: where do they learn to play the bull fiddle? Where do they practice it? Knowing as we do the sounds of young gentlemen doing their scales hour by hour on the piano, or young ladies, in the house across the street, doing their soprano scales, what kind of house do bull fiddlers live in, that they may grunt, groan and boom their practices by the hour?

It reminds me of the summer evening I was driving the family after supper in the rural backroads beyond the city limits when I spied, across a distant pasture, a lone figure of a man striding back and forth playing the bagpipe. I stopped the car and we listened to the far sweet sounds. It was "The Flowers of the Forest" he was playing, a lament. I got out and waded across the pastures and climbed the fences. As I approached, the piper desisted, and the bag gave that doleful groan it gives on deflation.

"Excuse me, sir," I said, "but am I intruding on some ceremony?"

"I am just practicin'," replied the Hielanman, stiffly.

"Ah, you live around here?"

"Na, Na," said he. "I live in toon, but ye canna practice in toon. I hae been flang oot o' four boardin' hooses in twa years. The woman says I am distairbin' the peace."

"Ah."

"The noo," said the piper, "I hae a fine wee room in a guid boardin' hoose and I come oot here tae practice."

"You will excuse me for intruding? When I heard 'The Flowers of the Forest,' I thought perhaps this was some ceremony. . . ."

"Na, na! I was juist practicin' it. But I will say I was thinkin' of a' the lads I knew."

"Soldier?"

"Yes, sirrr!"

I lifted my hat to him and retreated across the pasture, and we sat in the car and listened until darkness fell, and the music ended.

Scrabble

When we older people were being taught to spell, we learned that cuh-ah-tuh spelled cat, and that duh-aw-guh spelled dog. As we grew more advanced in our academic struggles, we came on words like tuh-huh aw-oo guh-huh that didn't make sense at all, but after a few experiences we learned that the word "though" was one of the tricks we would have to watch for.

The modern child is spared all the pitfalls of phonetics and teachers assure me that the art of spelling has not suffered, and that spelling matches today turn out better champions than they used to in my day.

But the game of scrabble is revealing a startling number of people who don't know how to spell. This game is sort of reverse crossword puzzle. You build words on a checkerboard. And if there is anything funnier than two people who can't spell playing scrabble, I would like to hear of it. I was called in to referee such a game. The lady who had opened had the word "bad" among the counters dealt her, and she set it down. The other lady, with a glad cry put down "bulit."

"What's that?" I checked.

"Bullet," said the player.

"That's not right," I laughed.

"What's the matter with it?" demanded her opponent, suspiciously. "That spells bullet."

So I sat back and let them go. Before the game ended, we had anser, adversory, fraim, revele, soket, thum, darector, and flebe.

"Flebe?" I could stand it no longer. "What's a flebe?"

"It's a kind of bird," said the lady who played it.

And since both of them knew of a bird named flebe, I figured scrabble a wonderful game. Everybody can play it.

Loris

It was with a distress almost childish that I learned a couple of years ago, from an ostrich breeder, that ostriches do not bury their heads in the sand when pursued by their enemies.

A fine world it will be, when all the myths and fables are exploded! Witches are gone, except in Britain and certain parts of the Southern states; werewolves, goblins, vampires, dragons, warlocks, banshees—all, all blown up like paper bags and burst in our faces. In the olden days, when the whole world consisted largely of small villages, I suppose they had to invent something to be afraid of. When you live in a village, there is nothing to be scared of so you make up fabulous monsters that dwell just over the mountains. To make life interesting, in a village, you have to invent dragons, werewolves, draculas.

The reason all these myths are being exploded is probably because now we have something to be afraid of, and don't need imaginary things. We have atomic bombs, death rays and inter-continental rockets. They are not myths. They are real. So out go your banshees and sea serpents, hexes and witches. The ostrich no longer hides his head in the sand. We do that now.

It is with a joy almost childish, however, that I now give you a fact, to which there are scientific witnesses, which puts the ostrich hiding its head entirely in the shade.

In India, there is a diminutive animal, about the size of a squirrel, called the loris. It is a member of the lemur family who are distant relatives of the monkeys, like us. Many scientists are inclined to believe that lemurs, by reason of their excessively slow and deliberate movements, as well as because of certain anatomical features, may be closer relations of ours than the monkeys.

The little loris is a nocturnal animal, and hides in the shrubbery catching flies and insects on the wing. It has a moist pinkish palm to its tiny hand, and it snatches its food with superb dexterity. How like the rest of us.

Now comes the part that beats the ostriches. When you approach a loris and when it realizes it has been discovered, it quietly covers its face with its hands!

If it can't see you, you can't see it. All hail to the little loris, who restores to us one of our fundamental fables.

Informed

Distinguished and famous men ought to be obliged to dress the part. In the olden days, it was difficult for a man to make a fool of himself, because all his betters wore the dress of their rank and station. Nowadays, you can't tell a millionaire from a union organizer. And in consequence, you can make some funny mistakes.

The French, who have a fine and tender social sense, recognize this situation; so they award their notable men the Legion of Honor, and in their buttonholes they wear the tiny civilian rosette of that order. You know you are talking to somebody, even if he doesn't look it.

In Britain, this is a fairly safe rule to follow: if he looks like somebody, he is sure to be nobody. But is the reverse true?

Across the table from me in what corresponds to the dining car in England sat a mild, meek Englishman who, after staring intently out the window for a while, ventured, to my amazement, that it was a fine day. He knew I was a Canadian or American by my speech when I spoke to the waiter, so I presumed his curiosity got the better of his English reserve. He was sorry I was not American, because he had been in America when he was a young man. I enquired what line he was in, over there. And after some thought, he suspected it might be the hotel business. He noted the two books I had on the table edge beside me, which were a couple of second-hand fishing books, one by Charles Kingsley entitled "New Miscellany." This turned our conversation to literature; and I expressed the opinion that there had been no literature in England, really, since about 1850. He seemed interested. I figured that this gentle, weary man—possibly a war plant executive on his way to a London conference—might welcome a little distraction. So I entertained him for an hour with a brilliant discourse on English literature. He took little part. He just listened.

Three men met him in the London station. The station master, in a plug hat, lifted his hat to my friend.

"Who is that?" I asked, after he had passed.

"Mr. John Masefield, the poet laureate," said the station master.

The Wink

In the restaurant, there was a family party at the next table to us: an elderly woman and six younger people, her children, obviously, and their wives and husbands. They were having a miserable time.

Mamma was playing duchess. She was rather a homey old gal, all dressed up for the occasion, which is a very mean description of the type who does not often get out socially. She had on her best hat, best coat. And you could see they were her best.

In a rather loud voice, she was instructing the waitress.

She explored the menu thoroughly, enquiring about various items. She suggested substitutions. She was having a whale of a time. She was behaving the way, in all her lonely hours, she had imagined ladies behaved in high society. She was entirely oblivious of the anguish of her children as she ladied it, which is the feminine of lorded it, over the waitress and all her company. It was intensely pathetic, a little conspicuous, and I caught the eye of one of her children. He gave me a sardonic wink.

Their party broke up when ours did, and we mixed at the hat check counter. The young fellow who had winked at me, drew me aside.

"Really," he said, "she is a wonderful old girl. We love her. But when she gets loose, like this, she's awful. She gets delusions of grandeur."

"Take her out oftener," I said.

For I don't like sardonic winks.

Preview

To my horror, a female member of our family circle, settling herself comfortably in a garden chair on the back porch and picking up a paperback murder mystery, calmly opened it at the back and began reading the last two or three pages.

"Good heavens, woman!" I cried.

"I always read the finish first," she replied.

"But you ruin the whole intention of the book," I protested. "The very purpose of a mystery story is to keep you in suspense."

"Not me," she declared. "I can't bear to be kept in suspense. So I read the end first, finding out who done it. This allows me the extra pleasure of being the only person present, other than the author, who really knows the solution of the mystery. It is mighty nice to know more than anybody else in the whole story, including the detective. As we go along, everybody all confused and bewildered, and the poor old detective floundering around trying to piece it together, there I am, all by myself, the only one in the know. It gives me a lovely feeling of intelligent superiority."

While I watched, spellbound, she read the last couple of pages; and then, looking very clever indeed, and with an air of great expectation, turned to the first page and launched into the tale.

The Critics

The art of trumpeting while blowing the nose is one of the manly arts that has almost died out. In the bus recently I heard a magnificent trombone tone, and on glancing behind, saw a young man dusting off his proboscis after having executed as fine a snort as I heard even in the early nineteen hundreds, when trumpeting was high style.

Indeed, there were really only two stages in a man's growth. One was when he moved out of short pants into long pants, around the age of fourteen. The other was when he succeeded in making a blast like a cornet with his nose when blowing; and this usually occurred around the age of twenty. By the time a man was forty, he was in his prime, and could sound off not only loud but long.

The Presbyterian church I attended as a boy was ministered unto by the Rev. Mr. Mutch. In his congregation was a sprinkling of elderly Scots who did not entirely hold with some of Mr. Mutch's doctrine. And when, during a sermon, there arose grounds for dissent, in various parts of the church would suddenly sound off these stentorian trumpets. No one could find fault with a gentleman blowing his nose. But I still see Mr. Mutch pausing in his discourse to glare at the congregation of whom only the very young giggled, having no proper conception of the contentious elements of theology.

Earache

A politician of my acquaintance lost a lot of ground in an area where he hoped to gain very important influences in his behalf. It all resulted from a banquet he attended, at which he was seated between two ladies, the wives of political celebrities. It was observed by many at the banquet that he paid much more attention to the lady on his right than to the one on his left. But to no one was this more apparent and more humiliating than to that quiet little lady on his left.

And the sad part of it is that the quiet little lady on his left was much the more important of the two, politically.

After the banquet, someone had the sagacity to mention the matter to the politician. He was horror-stricken.

"Why," he said, "I merely talked most to the one on my good ear side. I can hardly hear at all with my left ear; and she spoke so softly I hardly knew what she was saying. The other had a good loud voice . . ."

When this explanation was spread around, the lady who had been on his right heard it.

"Oh," she said, madder than the other lady, "so he thinks I am a loud talker, does he?"

To be a politician, I guess it is best to be deaf in both ears.

The Waker

As a guest in a friend's home, I was waked in the morning by strains of soft music. It was a clock radio by my bedside, no great novelty, but my first experience of it.

As I lay in comfort listening to the strains of Mendelssohn's Spring Song, I thought of the alarm clock my grandfather invented back in the eighteen sixties when he was in his prime as an inventor of collapsible easy chairs, suits of harness that would fall from the barn ceiling onto horses, and many other disastrous devices.

This alarm clock had the usual bell. But the spring activating the bell also wound up another spring in the process of running down. And when the bell ended, the other spring was released and a small hammer fell on a cap or primer such as was still used in those days for muzzle loading guns. This cap went off with a terrific bang, a fulminant quantity of smoke billowing out of the clock.

If this did not wake the sleeper, there was a brief pause, and then two spiral springs affixed to the legs of the clock came into operation, and the clock began a violent jigging motion which would certainly cause it to fall off the dresser or table on which it stood.

"But," protested my father, "It would smash!"

"No farmer," said my grandfather, the inventor, "would risk losing a clock worth six dollars. He would wake up."

But it never got past the planning stage.

The Hungry Bassos

Over the holidays, I heard a couple of Russian choirs on the radio. In this country, we go in for tenors. The Russians go in for bassos. And they seem to have a large supply of them with voices that go right down into their boots.

When, for example, they are singing a song about "The Dear Little Nightingale" the choir, in full voice like a pack of foxhounds with the fox in view, lets go altogether in magnificent harmony and choral power that Handel would have gone crazy over. It is roof-lifting.

So they sing, with explosions of tremendous violence, followed by beautifully muted passages, as they describe the Dear Little Nightingale.

And as the ballad progresses, you notice that the bassos are getting the better of the tenors and baritones. There comes, little by little, a sort of deep buzz into the music. That is the bassos taking over.

The ballad rises to its climax. The Dear Little Nightingale is described to its uttermost in a stupendous symphony of voices.

And as the ballad dies away, all you hear is the bassos in a long-drawn ooommmmmmmm. They have eaten the nightingale.

Zone of Quiet

Curling is referred to as the "roarin' game." I suspect this is one of those Scottish jokes. For a quieter game, unless it is tiddly-winks, you will seldom see. Since it is played now almost entirely in indoor rinks, there is a sort of hollow, echoing sound of rocks hitting each other, an occasional exclamation from a player that startles the empty rain barrel silence of the rink. The players wear rubber soled boots, so that even when they are scampering with their brooms, sweeping ahead of a rock, they make no sound. The swish-swish of the brooms is inaudible.

The players do not shout directions or encouragement from one end of the ice to the other. No. They signal with their brooms, the skips semaphoring with the utmost modesty and economy or gesture, where the next rock is desired.

Perhaps in the olden days, the Scots who conceived the game, as they did golf, may have hooted and hollered, out on the open-air rinks, from the invigorating effects of the cold and the tonic waters the Scots employed to ward off chill.

There was more roarin' at my old aunties' euchre parties than there is at a curling match.

Election Night at
Hyde Park

Every newspaperman treasures pet memories of his reporting days. (All publishers, managing directors and business managers of newspapers should have been reporters at some time in their careers, otherwise they don't know what it is all about.) My pet memory is of Franklin Delano Roosevelt, at his home in Hyde Parke, New York, sitting in a big leather chair, the collected works of Rudyard Kipling forming a background for his head.

I had been one of the lucky correspondents elected to sit with the President of the United States in his home during the reception of the election returns of his campaign for the presidency. It was the typical election night scene in the home of any candidate, whether an alderman or a president:

young ladies of the family and the neighborhood wandering about with platters of sandwiches, or a pitcher of coffee; the elder statesmen of journalism clustered around the great man, barring the approach of us small fry; Mrs. Eleanor Roosevelt, the president's wife, bustling about, seeing everybody was happy, and Mrs. Sarah Delano Roosevelt, the president's mother, looking us all over with astonishment.

It was the elder Mrs. Roosevelt I had my eye on. She may have been the mother of a president, of a famous man, but she was a very human old lady. Nobody was paying her court.

I paid her court.

And in a little while, she took my hand and we went up to Franklin, her boy, and burst through the serried ranks of the elder statesmen of journalism, and scattered them in all directions.

"Franklin," she said imperiously, "here is a friend of mine who wants to know what you think of Spain. Are you on the side of the republicans or of the fascists?"

The president looked at me with radiant understanding. I had been courting his mother. He motioned me to sit down with him, waving all the elder statesmen of the press away.

The president's mother sat down on the arm of my chair.

All I wanted, all I prayed for, was a photographer, to get the picture of Franklin Delano Roosevelt, his head thrown back, his eyes full of mischief and understanding, and the collected works of Rudyard Kipling behind his head there in the library of his house.

But what I got was something better.

"Mr. Clark," said the president of the United States, "I regret that I do not have sufficient information on which to base an opinion."

"Good boy," said Mrs. Sarah Delano Roosevelt.

And she took my hand and led me back into the melee.

The Door Opener

The late Frederick Griffin, one of Canada's ablest newspapermen, had a fiery Irish temper which made it difficult for him to abide policemen, officials, doorkeepers, secretaries and vice-presidents who stood between him and the man or the event he wished to see, first hand.

He could be quite stormy at times, and very often he was able to blow aside all adversaries trying to bar him from "the story."

But every now and then he would come up against somebody who stood fast against him, some police chief, some crown attorney, gateman, private secretary, colonel, brass hat. Griffin would literally weep with frustration.

He was in his forties when he made his great discovery. And I was with him at the moment.

A steamship official was trying to prevent us from getting aboard a rescue tug going out to the scene of a marine disaster. The official was rude, obscene and blasphemous, right in front of his female office staff.

"Thank you," said Griffin, to my astonishment. "Thank you, sir. I am a newspaperman. To me, everything that happens to me is a story. I am obliged to you for a very interesting few paragraphs."

We did not reach the door before the official, floundering with apologies, was begging us to sit down a minute.

We got on the tug all right. And Griffin had found the magic phrases that thereafter opened many a closed door.

To a newspaperman, everything that happens to him is a story.

The Press Room: Temple of Freedom

When we think of the freedom of the press in these modern times we naturally refer in our minds to the newspapers. The press, in present parlance, usually does mean the newspapers. But the press for whose freedom John Milton and a mighty parade of our noblest minds wrought and fought and languished in prison and died, was the machine—the printing press. And in our time, that goes for the huge plunging presses of the great dailies as well as for the little flatbed presses of the country weeklies. It refers to the intricate machines of the book printers and to the hand presses of the

142

printers of dodgers and tracts. We are a little inclined to forget that, even in the newspaper business. Thus it is a good thing for old editors to take young reporters by the scruff of the neck and lead them out back and make them look at the machine. That is the thing for whose freedom we live. It is, in a sense, an altar. And wherever on earth today it is desecrated, there is oppression, cruelty and death.

My father, who was a journeyman printer before he became an editor, used to take me with him, when I was a small boy, on his travels about the country. And whether in big cities or small villages, we invariably visited the newspaper offices. And never did these visits conclude without my old man asking to see the presses. And there he would stand, I am sure puzzling his friend the editor or country publisher, for a long minute, with a kind of glow on him.

It was a ritual with him. He was paying reverence to the machine. The machine that John Milton had in mind, the machine that disseminates the mind of man and puts it on the record.

I suppose the world is in greater political ruin today than it has ever been in history. How much of that ruin is due, in concrete example, to the enslavement of the press we may estimate according to our own information and conception. But not long ago I held in my hands a small fragmentary Hungarian newspaper, nothing but a handbill really. It was one of those printed by the ill-fated liberators.

It was printed badly. It must have come off a little, run-down press, perhaps in some village distant from Budapest.

What a good thing it would be, some day, to make a pilgrimage to that press, if only we could find it.

Whatever Happened to Lulu and Sophie and Bella and...

One of my nice nieces had a baby girl the other day and asked me what I thought of Jennifer for a name.

Jennifer! For Pete's sake. Jennifer is a variation of Guenevere. And what does Guenevere mean? A white phantom. We don't want any phantoms in our family.

"Look," I said to her. "Where are all the pretty names that were the fashion when I was young? Lulu. I haven't met a Lulu for thirty years.

"And Bella. The girl that sat next to me in the First Book, was named Bella. And what a nice girl she was. And I can remember the names of the other girls in my class. There was a Nellie and two Bessies, a Violet, two Annies, a Sadie, a tall, thin Olive, two Roses, a fat one and a little eeny, weeny skinny one; there was Ruby, the teacher's pet, and Minnie."

"Gahhh!" said my niece.

"Sophie!" I cried. "There was a Sophie lived next door to us. Then across the street there were three sisters, Abby, Lola and Etta. What on earth has happened to all the pretty

144

names of yesterday? What happened to that Bella I knew in school, what happened to the Lulus and the Daisies and the Nellies? Didn't they become Aunt Bella and Aunt Lulu and Aunt Sophie? And if they became aunts, what kind of aunts did they become, if no one ever named a baby in this generation after them?"

My niece was sorry for me, so she explained that no doubt Lulu became Louise by the time she grew up, and Etta grew up to be Henrietta, and Annie became Anne, and Nellie went back to Helen, and so forth.

"Okay, then," I said firmly. "How about Bella?"

They compromised by calling the new baby Heather.

Bruno

A cousin of mine has a dog, of great character but undeterminable breeding, which has almost human intelligence. Or so they say.

His greatest attribute is that he is very fond of children. And wonderful stories are told of his tireless devotion to the little ones in the family. He never lets them out of his sight. Where they go, he goes.

His prime performance is watching the new babies in their baby carriages out in front of the house. There he lies, the perfect watchdog, never taking his eyes off the baby.

From the hammock one summer day I was watching old

Bruno standing guard over the baby, who was put out for a little air after its siesta. As is usual, the baby, being ten months old, is given a bikkie to gnaw at whilst taking the sun.

Old Bruno, that faithful animal, came dutifully along, close beside the carriage as it was wheeled out. And when it was locked in place, he slumped down beside it, the picture of a grand old soldier on sentry duty.

When everybody but me had returned to the house, Bruno gazed watchfully about. He studied me, in the hammock, for a long minute or two. I feigned sleep. When Bruno was satisfied that nobody was looking, he got casually to his feet. He made the rounds of the baby carriage, peering in all directions.

Then, assured of privacy, he rose up on his hind legs and robbed the baby of its bikkie.

Bruno, it seems, is fond of children for the simple reason that they eat oftener than adults. You never can tell, in the prosperous company of children, when some goodie is going to be available. The pickings are far better with kids than with grown-ups.

I got up and went in the house and got a new arrowroot. I gave it to the baby, who was properly grateful, and then returned to the hammock, and soon was wrapped in apparent slumber. Dear old Bruno, glancing absently about while I presented the biscuit to the baby, resumed his faithful post by the carriage, his chin resting on his paws, the picture of impersonal devotion. After about five minutes, by which time the baby had just gummed the edges of the biscuit, old Bruno cautiously raised his head and scanned me long and steadily. Reassured, he got to his feet, went around to the far side, rose up and robbed the baby the second time.

"Harrayah" I roared.

Outraged, he went and slunk under the porch and stayed there, brooding.

Dugald

The most dogged of all dogs is the Scottish terrier. Harsh coated, dour, low down to the ground and bandy legged, he has built up the reputation of being a one-man dog. More than that, he has been smart enough to kid everybody in whatever family he condescends to live with that he is a one-man dog to him or her and nobody else.

Some friends of mine have one named Dugald. And there was a terrible hue and cry one day when Dugald failed to come home for supper. Dugald was lost. It is astonishing a grip a dog can take on the hearts of a family. It was as if someone in the family were missing.

They hunted and they scoured. They called the Humane Society and the police. But for two long melancholy days, there was no word. Then the Humane Society telephoned to say somebody had brought in a Scotty.

"Has he a grey wisp between his eyes?" the family begged.

"Aye, he has," agreed the Humane Society man, already adopting the Scottish burr.

Rejoicing, the family drove madly down to the Humane Society. They rushed upon Dugald.

But Dugald, withdrawing frigidly as only a Scotty can, ignored the family. It was obvious he had never laid eyes on them before. Not merely did he not wag a tail. He detached himself from their embraces and sat apart by himself.

"But it IS Dugald!" the family insisted. "That grey wisp between the eyes . . .!"

The Humane Society man was very regretful. But he

could not hand the dog over unless it was positively identified. Finally, after much pleading, the family was allowed to take the Scotty home until the rightful owner called.

All the way home, the Scotty stared indifferently at the family and then, more indifferently, out the car window. At home they led him triumphantly back into the familiar scenes. The Scotty, with dignity, explored the place; then sat apart, near the door. It was supper time before Dugald finally relented. All of a sudden, he got up and ran down to the cellar and came back up with his tin feeding dish!

Having suffered the indignity of getting lost, Dugald felt he had to take it out on somebody.

Kindergarten Rock

A very young friend of mine has started to kindergarten, and since I have shared various exciting experiences with him, such as catching frogs, climbing trees, seeing the aurora borealis (which got us both into hot water for taking him out of bed at midnight), he felt it was only decent that he should share this newest adventure with me. So he came over and invited me to go to school with him next morning to hear the band.

"It's a riddum band," he explained, practically incandescent with excitement. "All the girls and boys. We make all the noise we want. I have got a mallick."

"Uh-huh?" I enquired.

"I hit a box with the mallick. Wow!"

"Are you supposed to?" I checked.

"I've got to!" he announced with considerable incredulity. "The box is holla. And the teacher says to me, hit it, hit it! And I sit right there and hit it. With the mallick!"

We stared at each other, finding it a little hard to believe.

"The teacher plays the piano. And she nods her head. And some have sticks, and some have bells and iron sticks, and everything makes a noise. And when the teacher nods her head, we all have got to hit whatever it is as hard as we can. Will you come?"

I said I sure would.

So off to school we went, and the teacher was very pleased to see me and got me a larger chair on account of my width. And she provided me with a mallick and a holla box, just like my friend's. And when she played "Do Ye Ken John Peel" on the piano and nodded the time to us, we all beat the stuffing out of bells, triangles, rods, jinglers, whangers, clickers, drums, and the darndest assortment of musical instruments I ever saw.

"How long has this been going on?" I asked the teacher when I got the chance.

"Oh, for years and years. The rhythm band is an old established feature of kindergarten work."

"Well, for heaven's sakes!" I cried. "And here I've been wondering for the past fifteen years where the younger generation got its taste in music."

Prisoners of June

This is strictly for the eyes of young people of school age. It seems monstrous that in beautiful June, the agony and woe of examinations could be visited upon the only decent people in the world—the young. Exams should be held during the filthiest week of February, when it certainly isn't fit to go skiing, and hardly fit to go out to a movie. In all nature, spring is not a time of testing, of auditing, of accounting and summing up. Spring is seeding time, nesting time, time for song and love and joy.

I address myself to those of you who are failing or have failed. And this is strictly between you and me. If you fail, it may be because you are equipped for a joyous, colorful eventful life, with all the best characteristics that life can bestow on mortals. Maybe you could not keep your mind on your work, because, outside the classroom windows the sun shone, the green boughs waved and the wide sky was blue. Maybe all the dull statistics you have been pouching in your mind these past many weeks all seemed to melt and vanish, as you sat there at the examination desk, because your body and soul was being called away, called away, by vast intangible nameless forces, singing to you.

Someday soon you will know that it is better to be alive than clever, sensitive than informed, perceptive than erudite —better to be you than anybody you can think of.

Honor Milne

Honor Milne was a teacher handicapped by very poor vision and she wore enormously thick spectacles. She taught first grade. And it was a matter of concern in the schools she taught in that there was always a terrible racket in her classes. "But," as the principals used to say, "what can we do about it? She passes the children with higher grades than the rest of you."

Soon there was to be added a new racket to her class rooms. Sixty years ago, she began seeking out the crippled children of her diocese, so to speak, and teaching them after hours and in her evenings. When her hands became too full, she persuaded the school authorities to allow the older boys to bring the crippled children to her classes. So the thump of crutches, the rattle and crash of leg braces joined the joyful tumult of Honor Milne's classrooms. And still the grades grew higher, finer. She lived to see, and to teach in, schools specially dedicated to the crippled.

Not by argument, not by organization, but by single-handed demonstration, this shy, gentle woman pioneered the schools for crippled children that today are recognized everywhere as part of the normal educational program of cities.

To see Honor Milne on the street, peering through her thick lenses, moving shyly, cautiously, and wearing that eternal smile that those of poor vision wear lest they fail to smile at a friend, you would never suspect her of being the great liberator that she was until she died in Toronto in her eightieth year.

When she lay in state before her funeral, the most tremendous moment was when her alumnae, grown men and women, some in middle age, came with their crutches, sticks, braces, to say farewell. They were representative of the thousands Honor Milne had liberated from the prison in which the crippled had once lived.

December Demonics

Are there now signs that the Santa Claus mania is peaking? In a department store I have seen a woeful sight. There on his throne in the toy department sat Santa Claus, a figure of majesty in scarlet and white. He was surrounded by scenic splendor, in which toys of great price, together with toys of very modest price indeed, were skilfully displayed about him. This demonstrates the true democratic character of dear old Santa Claus. He can accommodate the dreams of childhood in practically any price class. Up the ramp leading to his throne filed a procession of very small children whose parents stood in the throng waiting at either end of the ramp, all lost in tremulous delight at the beautiful spectacle of infant delusion.

Suddenly the procession halted. A little girl of about three years of age was next in line for the great moment. She hung back, clutching the railing of the ramp. Then she burst into wild screams of terror. She could not back up, because of the solid queue of children behind her. To go forward, she would have to pass the awful ogre she beheld square in front of her.

What an ogre it was! A vast stuffed ogre, clad in scarlet, its face hidden by a ghastly jungle of fur, out of which two wild eyes peered. Even as she screamed, the little girl saw the ogre reaching out its arms for her, and it half rose from its throne to get at her. My sympathies were all with the little girl. An imaginary Santa Claus is spooky enough. A real stuffed one is more gruesome than a stuffed moose. Her screeches were electric. Suddenly, all the children behind her on the ramp caught the infection. And dear old Santa Claus was surrounded by howling, screaming childhood, madly tumbling backwards off the ramp and down to the safety of their mothers' arms.

Christmas Rose

Well, it seems that when those camels with their jangling bells came through the dirty old back streets and down to the stable back of the inn, they attracted quite a crowd. And when the three Magi descended, and walked stooping into the stable with their gifts, there crowded right behind them, amid all the pushing and shoving, a small girl.

She must have been about eight, or perhaps ten.

At any rate, she was past the age when small girls largely want things. She had reached the age when she had the first strong stir of giving, which is characteristic of her sort.

And when, among that sudden glory and stillness, the Magi knelt on the soiled ground and held up their gifts, gold, frankincense and myrrh, the little girl happened, naturally, to be right in the front row.

And there she was, with nothing to give. But this is the Legend of the Rose, and it goes back to the eleventh or even the tenth century. So we must give it as it comes, for who are we to say what is legend?

When she saw the gifts of the Magi, all glowing, she was suddenly aware. Sooner or later, we are all aware that we have nothing to give. But she was only eight, or maybe ten. And the tears welled in her eyes, ran down her cheek, fell on the ground.

And in that eternal moment of great stillness, out of the soiled ground, exactly where her tears had dropped, there came a small crackling and a whispering, and a small green leaf appeared, and then a stem, and then a bush and then, a rose. And the legend goes that even the Magi lowered their hands, and stood back.

That is the legend of the Christmas Rose, carols are wound around it, it is told in all the tongues.

The meaning of it we can choose for ourselves. But it has to do with those who suppose that they have nothing to give, on Christmas Day.

Uncle Rafe

My old Uncle Rafe did not go to church, but he was a very animated Christian who could argue the Bible with all comers. Christmas was to him a season of jubilation. A week before Christmas, much to the chagrin of all his relatives, he would join the wandering bands of the Salvation Army and, though a very indifferent player upon the trombone, would add his music to theirs through the wintry nights. He also enjoyed Salvation Army singing, and if, in the midst of a purely instrumental rendering of Holy Night you heard, one night, a sort of rain barrel baritone suddenly take up the words, that would have been Uncle Rafe lowering his trombone and vocalizing.

If the Anglicans were putting on a pre-Christmas cantata, Uncle Rafe would be there, in the front row of the audience, so that he could join in without being conspicuous. He was particularly fond of Handel, whom he called the Holy Cheer Leader.

Anglican or Baptist, Presbyterian or Methodist, Uncle Rafe had no bigotry. So long as they jubilated at Christmas, he was with them body and soul. And never did he miss midnight Christmas mass at the Roman Catholic cathedral. To him, as he said, that put the icing on it.

Uncle Rafe did not give lavish gifts to us, or to any of his numerous friends. He usually gave me a 25 cent bandanna handkerchief.

"Use it, boy," he would say. "A man looks ridiculous twiddling behind those white doilies they sell as hankies."

But without fail, he always bought three more gifts than his Christmas list called for. Three. Always three.

"You never know," he said, "who you forgot. And to forget, on Christmas, would be terrible. Remember, son, they had to lay Him in a manger. Watch out for the Stranger, Christmas day."

Thus, at daybreak, Christmas morn, Uncle Rafe would be out on his front steps watching for the first three Strangers who might go by, the milkman, a paperboy, or some besodden reveller coming home at dawn.

And on them, Uncle Rafe would press his three extra gifts of Christmas, a red handkerchief, a pair of pretty candles, an aluminum saucepan done up in white tissue with lovely ribbon. Small, odd gifts, but Uncle Rafe was a small odd man, with a leaning to personal jubilation.

Tuning Out

Being really deaf is quite an encumbrance. But being slightly deaf has its advantages. One of my eardrums was ruptured in the first war and the other was damaged when I was a young reporter by attending too many service club meetings and having to listen. Honest wear and tear, my ear specialist says. He hits me on the head with a sort of tuning fork with a knob on it and asks me do I hear anything. He repeats numbers half under his breath, meanwhile backing away from me and asking me to repeat them after him. It is like reading those smaller letters on the chart at the eye specialist's. I don't hear anything, but I think of a number anyway and give it to him.

"Do you notice any decline in your hearing?" he enquires.

"You bet," I assure him. "It's wonderful at the movies. I can't quite make out what the actors are saying, but I don't hear those two women in the seat behind me either. And I haven't heard any kids munching popcorn or old bachelors chewing humbugs in five years."

"Aha," says the ear specialist. "And how about telephone bells?"

"We had the bells taken out at our house fifteen years ago," I explain, "and replaced by buzzers. You can only hear the buzzers when you are quite near the phone, which saves running all over the house."

"Do you still hear them?"

"Nobody calls me up anymore," I explain.

"Look," he says. "You're losing your hearing!"

"I can still hear what I want to hear," I counter.

"Birds?" he asks.

"Modern robins," I assured him, "don't sing the way they did in the old days. The way I remember robins singing is far ahead of the way they sing nowadays."

"Whippoorwills?"

"Very tiresome they used to be."

"Music?"

"I turn it up loud," I revealed, referring of course to the radio and the record player. "Some of the high notes are a little scratchy, and the bass notes mumble a bit. But music is in the heart. You remember how it ought to be. These present day musicians only work on symphony on Sundays or when making recordings. Can they be expected to be as good as they were thirty years ago?"

"Can anybody?" agrees the specialist, hitting me on the head again with his knobbed tuning fork.

Counting

After you pass sixty years of age, you get furtive thoughts, no matter how cheery you may me, that run, like little mice, amid the rafters of your mind.

When I was a young man courting my wife, I used to count the telephone poles along the street, as I walked to her house, to tell me, by their being odd or even, whether I was going to get a friendly reception or a chilly one. I was a homely little freckled guy, always in expectation of chills.

If I remember, even meant warm, odd meant chill.

When, in course of time, I got to know the telephone poles so well I could cheat, I decided the manly thing would be to trust the cracks in the concrete sidewalk. But even these became too familiar for truth. By the time I won my bride, I had run out of all signs and tokens that would guide me into the immediate future.

Now that I am coming along, in years, somewhere near the end of all pavements and telephone poles, I have suddenly caught myself at the old tricks. Do you suppose it is my youth returning?

Going upstairs, a little puffy, I find myself wondering if, in the Islamic tradition of fate, this is the hundredth to last or the thousandth to last time I am to walk up stairs. I bought some razor blades the other day, quite a quantity of them on sale, and on opening the package and counting them, I detected myself wondering: "Is this the measure? Am I to use them up; and then, no more?"

Morbid thoughts? Never. Just natural curiosity, a curiosity I never experienced even as a young man marking the passage of the hours in the trenches of Arras or Ypres. But once past sixty, your curiosity is liable to be aroused.

Sometimes, in the very old, you glimpse an enigmatic expression in their eyes.

It is a distant look, stilled, expectant, shy, sly, half whimsical, seldom afraid.

I know what they are up to.

They are counting.

Reprieve

An aged lady of my acquaintance has had a very trying year. One by one, her few remaining close friends and relations have passed away. Of course, at her age, they have been dying off for twenty years. But there comes a time in a person's life when the number of those remaining becomes so small that it begins to feel as if a finger were pointing.

And this dear old lady began to be conscious of that pointing finger.

"I'll be next," she declared hollowly, when, in the past few months, three of her cronies went, one, two, three.

So sure was she that she began to sit as if waiting. She could not get her mind off it. In her favorite rocking chair, she would rock a while and then suddenly stop, to announce:

"I'm next."

This became a little exhausting to her family, as well as most injurious to the old lady herself. Her health began to fail, as if indeed her turn had come.

Then, one of her nieces sent her a three-year subscription to her favorite magazine.

The trick worked like magic.

"Three years!" she says, waving the magazine. "My goodness!"

It must be somebody else who's next.

The Silencers

On recently being equipped, for the first time, with a fine set of false teeth, I was dismayed to discover my whistle was gone. It seems the dental profession can make a beautiful match for the teeth they deprive you of. But they cannot guarantee your whistle.

With my whistle, I could call a whippoorwill to my very feet. Out of the spring night, a whippoorwill would come a quarter of a mile or more to perch, in some astonishment, on the veranda railing, to join me in a robust duet. Indians regarded me as one who almost spoke their own language whenever I regaled them with this trick. Now I am reduced to one language again.

Chickadees, crested flycatchers, Baltimore orioles, the hermit thrush, meadow lark, and two kinds of hawk were on speaking terms with me when I had my old familiar teeth, every crack and crevice of which I knew with a curious intimacy—an intimacy that I do not enjoy with my hands or any other part of my anatomy. Teeth are intensely personal.

Not only birds but dogs are now all but lost to me. With a particular unmusical but intensely high-pitched whistle that was almost a hiss, I could halt a dog in his tracks at a hundred yards. Now I have to bellow; and bellowing is not good for a man of false teeth age. For taxicabs, there is nothing left now but to wave and gesticulate. Some young aspiring dentist might build for himself a select but lucrative practice by inventing a kind of false teeth with little holes in them for enabling whistling men to emit various beautiful blasts.

The Survivors

As you grow older, you go to more and more funerals. This is logical, I suppose. It is also no doubt logical that your view of your fellow mourners should be changed. A few years ago, when I went to only two or three funerals a year, I used to fume and fret because it appeared to me that funerals were just another of the social occasions. My tender sensibilities were outraged at the sight of elderly people greeting each other warmly in the funeral parlor and huddling off into corners in little groups with all the appearance of guests at a cocktail party. Right in the chapel itself, while we awaited the appearance of the clergyman amid the solemn sounds of a soft organ playing some seemly tune and the sight if not the scent of the heaped floral tributes, we would see some old turkey, cock or hen, walking up the aisle, after viewing the late departed, and shaking hands with folks in every other pew. Those who had not the nerve to do that were at least craning their necks to see who was present, and who was just coming in.

But the years soften us. After we get on the down slope of the sixties, a funeral is the occasion for seeing who's left. We are not greeting each other when you see us warmly shaking and huddling off into little cliques. We are congratulating each other on still being here.

But there are exceptions. I encountered an old friend on the street yesterday and remarked with some astonishment that I thought he would be at the funeral which was then taking place, of an old buddy of his.

"No," he said, cheerily, "he won't be at my funeral. Why should I be at his?"

Little Things

One of my friends was recently taken ill and there were some fears that it might be his end. He asked for me to come and see him to discuss his affairs, which flattered me because I am not much of a business head.

"No, no," he said from his sick bed. "My business affairs are in good shape, my will and all that. It isn't that that frets me. It is all the little things. Who is going to attend to putting water in the humidifiers on the radiators every few days when I'm gone? Who is going to check that expansion tank up in the attic that keeps the level in the heating system? Who's going to remember where the dog's license is? Who's going to change the fuses in the fuse box? Nobody else knows how.

"There are a thousand things. I keep lying here and thinking of all those little things that somebody will have to look after. Will they remember the name of the little fellow who repairs the panes in the downstairs leaded windows? Who will know what all those keys fit that are in my desk there. They can't possibly know. . . ."

So I wrote down at his dictation all the little things of his big life, and he got better, and we put my memorandum in the strong box with his will.

The Whistler

My Grandma had the habit or mannerism of softly and tonelessly whistling as she went about her work. There was no actual whistle to it, just a faint sibilance. As she baked cookies or sewed or even as she walked about the house, you could always hear the soft and tuneless murmur of this whisper of a whistle. Sometimes you could catch the rhythm or cadence of a tune, such as "Bringing in the Sheaves," or "Darling Nellie Grey" and we children used to love to get close to her, on the arm of her rocker, perhaps, and attempt to identify the tiny tuneless tunes with which she so absently entertained herself.

We children loved it. If we were ill, and Grandma was in the dim-lit room preparing a stocking full of heated salt for a sore throat, or watching over our restless slumber with a small dish of onion syrup, made of brown sugar melted on sliced onions, to give us for the croup or the whooping cough when the paroxysms waked us, it was a deep and penetrating pleasure to hear that eternal and lovely little murmur of Grandma's mannerism, there close beside us.

Grandma's daughters did not like this mannerism. They often spoke sharply to the old lady, asking her for heaven's sake to cease her whistling. And Grandma would desist for a little while, until she forgot, and went on with her little formless tune again. Often, her daughters did not have to speak; just a sharp jerk of their heads, and Grandma would close her lips firmly, with a contrite expression.

In the streetcar lately, a man sitting beside me reading a newspaper gave me a sudden, sideways jerk of a glance. I found myself closing my lips firmly, and feeling extremely contrite. And all the rest of the way home, I remembered Grandma with a sense of extraordinary reality.

164

Spring

There is a post box half way between my house and the bus stop. In one hand I carried three letters to post. In the other, I held my bus tickets which I had just taken from my pocket.

On reaching the post box, I posted my bus ticket, hurried across the street to catch the coming bus, and earnestly tried to stick my three letters in the bus fare box.

It is spring. It could be young men post bus tickets at this time of year. But I think it is more the elderly whom spring affects in this fashion.

You feel the spring. Its tremulous, loitering beauty wakens memories rather than utters promises. Indeed, it sometimes buries you so deep in memories that you grow a little absent in the mind. Posting bus tickets is by no means the worst of it. I hurried downstairs this morning, and when I got there, I forgot what it was I came down for. It is rather unnerving to have to stand there, in the living room, with a daffy smile on your face, trying to recollect what it was that sent you hustling downstairs with such purpose. It is just spring.

Last evening, in the rain, when the smell of the earth was coming in the open windows so wafty, I answered the telephone, and a gentleman asked if I were in. I regretted to tell him I was out. It was not until I hung up that I realized I was in, after all. Where was I, at that instant?

Far back, friends, maybe forty years away.

The Cloud Watcher

The day had cleared in mid-afternoon, following three dreary days of rain and wind. Everybody felt better. Now for a spell of fine weather.

Evening fell swiftly, as it does in October, and soon the sky was ablaze with stars. Like countless others, we planned a day in the open for tomorrow and began figuring a course in the country, where we might see the most of those wayside stands along the farm roads, and smell the aroma of stout autumn. But the oldest of us went to the veranda, gazed out for a moment and then came in.

"Rain tomorrow," he stated. "The stars are dripping."

We went with him to look. The stars were literally dripping with their light. We felt we had never seen them so resplendent.

And sure enough, when tomorrow came, it was with rain and wind again, like the whole week past. Dripping stars are one of the surest of weather signs. There are people, like this domestic prognosticator we have in our family, who know a great many indications of what the weather will be within a few hours, such as overnight.

"It is a matter of paying attention," he says. "We could all be weather prophets if we just looked and remembered, the direction of the wind, the height and the shape of clouds. I realize that there are air masses moving, far off, as the TV and radio weather men show us. But when the wind is in the west, and low clouds are sailing by, and you see, in the southeast, high clouds fanning out in your direction, you can be reasonably sure that tomorrow the wind will have changed to that direction. And if, in your country, the east brings rain, it will be rainy. Weather is seldom as surprising as it is supposed to be, if you form the habit of noting the perfectly obvious indications, and remember to check them the next day. It takes practice. You have to make a little hobby of it. Sailors and farmers have been practicing it for countless generations. It is more fun than listening to the weather report. And pretty near as accurate."

The Six Seasons

I would like to express thanks on behalf of all people as daft as myself to the Canadian Bank of Commerce and all others who give us calendars with two months on a sheet.

In June, for instance, my calendar, with a pretty rural landscape on it, shows the two months, May-June, side by side. Two lovely months. May is gone, and June is going. But there, at a glance, I see the lovely expanse of them, their whole sixty-one joyous, shimmering days. It is as if they were joined together, and set apart. They are a season unto themselves.

I tear off May and June. And there before my eyes are July and August, the full summer, the holiday season, and its entire sixty-two days, all spread out in one long, glorious glance. We can see it coming. We can watch it going. There will be no tearing off, midway of it. No surgical division of summer. The calendar will show us summer all summer through.

I realize there are other calendars that show the months fore and aft, with this month in bold-face type, and last month and next month in smaller type. But this is not half so heartening as the two months to a sheet style of calendar.

It gives our year in its natural twosomes. For in Canada, at any rate, our year does divide into twin months. We have July and August, united in spirit and in meteorology, the holiday season. Then we have September and October, twins in spirit and in feeling. Next come the iron twins, November and December. They are enlightened by the coming of Christmas, it is true. The sere and yellow leaf of November

168

first is balanced by the bright baubles and fictitious bright leaves of Christmas.

But the moment Christmas is over, up come the next twins, January and February. There is no dividing them. They are identical, whether you look at them from the gloomy viewpoint of the elderly, watching the blizzards and trembling on the icy pavements, or from that of the young, who think of skiing, or skating, or hockey or sleighs.

Finally, come March and April, both of which are blessed with the thought and the living expectation of spring. In March you see the tulip tips peeping. In April, you see the buds on the trees. March and April are a pair.

So here's to all donors of calendars who see the year not as a tabulation of twelve stiffly marching months, but as six seasons, each with a character and an individuality, each bearable because it is comprehensive and comprehensible.

All Our Shining Lustra

Everybody knows what a decade is. A ten-year period. The word comes in very handy for all sorts of conversation and communication and for the official, impersonal measurements of our gains and losses as compiled by politicians and the Dominion Bureau of Statistics.

But there is a far handier word than decade, and you hardly ever hear it used. It is lustrum. A lustrum is a period of five years.

It seems to me that our lives are better divided into lustra, as the plural of lustrum is, than into decades.

In our first lustrum, we are infants. But in our second lustrum, from five to ten, we become boys and girls. In our third lustrum, we enter our wonderful teens, and begin to become people. And in our fourth, we grow up.

From there on, how much easier it is to measure off our lives in lustra than in decades. A decade is a formless, featureless span of time, as far as our swifty-moving little destinies are concerned. Take war, for instance, Wars usually last one lustrum. For example, the lustrum before a war bears no earthly resemblance to the lustrum of the war itself. And the lustrum after a war is unique. It is the lustrum in which a young man, re-made or ruined by war, resumes normal life, in which a young woman adapts herself to some young man re-made or ruined by war.

So it goes. The fourth decade of a person's life is from age thirty to forty. Yet, like the third decade, it too is filled with events so diverse, so contrasting, so up and so down, so charged with fate for good or ill, that only the lustra can properly compass them; the seventh and eighth lustra.

Life fits most easily into packages of five years.

It is more fun to have twelve or fourteen lustra than five or six decades, or even seven.

A decade in our lives is a dark, formless thing.

A lustrum of it, any lustrum, has a character all its own.

June 30

Today, the year is half gone.

Tomorrow, we start on the down-slope. In nine weeks it will be September. And from there on in, the year skids through ever-darkening weeks to its close.

It never feels like a turning-point on June 30. It feels like a beginning. School is out, the holiday season has begun for adults as well as children. It seems like the start of all that we have waited for throughout the year.

At no other moment of the year does time seem to stretch away ahead of us with such a far horizon. On New Year's day, which we celebrate so earnestly and hopefully, there is a feeling that the back of winter is already broken, and after a few brief weeks of snow, a change will come, and spring will be sounding faint and not too far. In October, Christmas beckons us on, and time flies fast. From the first breath of spring until the end of June, the days fairly zip past us. But on June 30, time seems to stand still. Ahead of us stretches a great, long summer, a season with little visible change except the enrichment of the colors of the fields and a grow-ing heaviness of the trees. On June 30, it is impossible to think ahead, past or beyond what we now have. This is it. This is what all the twistings and turnings of time and season have wrought for.

It is an illusion. The year, tonight at midnight, is half gone. And all the things we promised ourselves for this twelve months should be half done, and most likely aren't.

And the more fools we if, on this occasion, we attempt to hold a half-yearly audit and make of life a matter of debit and credit. July is at the door. And after it comes August. And the sun will glow, and the trees wave for joy, and the wind blow in the time of year for which life itself seems to have been designed.

September

In the country, among homely people who believed in horse liniments and almanacs, there was a belief that you felt best in the month of your birth.

If you were born in lovely May or ominous November or grisly March, it did not matter. Whatever month you were born in was your big month, your healthiest, your most spirited, merry, prosperous.

Being a September bird myself, I must confess that September fills me with a terrific zest unparalleled in any other month of the year. But after a fairly extensive and long-continued enquiry among the kind of people who notice such things as how they feel and when, it appears that a great many feel this way about September; and many of them were born in such inspiring months as December and June. Part of the zest of September may originate in the weather, the hale winds, the brightening color, a sharpening. Some of the zest may come of the satisfaction of full barns, the harvest in, the cattle fat, the sheep grown, the hogs ripe for the cauldron.

But it seems to me some of this September zest is very ancient and very deep in our natures. Two thousand or a thousand years ago, September was the season all men remembered winter, and reached for their weapons. The caves, the huts had to be stored with the meat of the chase, venison dried and hung high in the smoke; fresh hides and furs to be gathered and cured for clothing and foot covering. The young game was grown, the old game was fat and prime.

Even the mildest and most humane, every living soul of us today is the descendant of a mighty hunter. For if you were not a good hunter, a successful killer, you didn't survive. When you see some flushed and spectacled member of the milder sort gleefully inhale the tang of September, reflect for a moment on the vulgar origins of that glee.

New Year's 1900

It is hard to convey, here late in the century, what a decorous occasion New Year's was in Canadian cities and towns one normal lifetime ago. Only the rich and the poor whooped it up New Year's Eve. The large stolid, solid majority, the good, virtuous, sternly self-respectful middle class, neither rich nor poor, owning neither horse and carriage nor horse and wagon, what we might call the pedestrian Canadians of 1900, might struggle to keep awake until midnight, so as to go to their front doors and listen to the far-off factory whistles hooting, and the bells of a few of the more flagrant churches (that went in for bells) clanging frostily.

But for the most part, they went to bed around ten, as usual. For it was New Year's Day that was the big event.

We dressed on New Year's Day as if for Sunday. By ten in the morning, the streets were as busy as if it were actually the Sabbath. The same family groups in their Sunday best walking purposefully. For New Year's Day was the day for visiting. The well-to-do, in their personal carriages or sleighs and the comfortable, in their hired livery cabs, trotted briskly. And, amid this scene of purposeful animation, we pedestrian families made our calls, on selected neighbors, on relations, on the parson, on the employer.

It went on from ten until five in the New Year afternoon.

And already half stuffed with Christmas cake and ginger snaps, we all went home to the sumptuous New Year's dinner which the maid had prepared.

The New Year was becomingly launched.

174

Countdown to Spring

My Grandma always loved the onset of winter.

"Now," she would say, "we can think of spring!"

In autumn, however drear, you can't really look forward to spring because first winter has to come. The early part of autumn has its glory. Indeed many of us prefer the early part of October, with its color, its soft haze, its sense of fruitful climax, to any other part of the year. But before October ends, most of us would like to start thinking of spring if we dared.

But we don't dare. It is too soon. Winter is icumen in.

When winter clamps down, like an iron door overhead and an iron floor underneath, we seize upon Christmas to cheer us with a gay traditional festival to try to tide us through. In former times we invented sleighs and festooned them with sleighbells and built up a whole literature of song and story celebrating the crispness, the chaste beauty, the merriment of winter. But while our noses ran and our hands chapped and we stumbled about in clumsy clothes amid the blizzards and the slush, the only really truly thing that kept us happy was the knowledge that spring comes next.

And from the dark December solstice, it is only ninety-two short days to the first day of spring when robins will be on the rooftops.